A Geography of Population:
World Patterns

A Geography of Population:
World Patterns

GLENN T. TREWARTHA

University of Wisconsin
Madison, Wisconsin

JOHN WILEY & SONS, INC.

New York   London   Sydney   Toronto

Cartography supervised by
Randall D. Sale

CONTENTS

Introduction

This small volume on the geography of human population in its broad, worldwide patterns is the first book of a planned trilogy on population geography. It is hoped that the separate parts eventually will be brought together into a single, comprehensive volume. The present book is topical in approach and stresses world patterns; the second and third will be regional in organization. Part 2 in the series will focus on population in the economically less developed regions. The peoples, mainly of European stock, who populate the scientifically and economically advanced nations will be the topic of Part 3. Part 1 forms a fairly complete entity and can thus be put to use during those several years that must elapse while the other two parts are slowly taking form.

If there were a unanimity of agreement on the content and methods of geography in general, a definition of population geography would present little problem. But the degree of accord granted the concept that geography in general is essentially concerned with the spatial distributions of things on the earth's surface allows us to call population geography the study of the spatial variations in human population. To be sure, this involves not only numbers but also population characteristics, as well as growth and mobility. The concept will be further elaborated in the pages to follow.

It is appropriate to raise the question concerning the relation of population geography to demography. Formal demography in its narrow sense is the science of vital statistics—birth, deaths, expectation of life, marriages, etc.—of human populations. It concentrates on the gathering, collating, statistical analysis, and presentation of population data. Such work demands technical skills, sometimes relatively sophisticated ones. Experts in the demographic techniques were once found mainly in government bureaus and life insurance companies. Gradually, however, demography has more and more come to be thought of as a synonym for general population study, with many of its practitioners now on university faculties, mainly in sociology and economics departments. The geography of population (or population geography) is concerned

1

chiefly with one aspect of population study—its spatial distributions and arrangements. Of course, it is both descriptive and explanatory. While demographers have by no means renounced the study of spatial variations of population, it is not one of their main areas of concentration.

Population geography has emerged as a distinctive and well recognized branch of geography only during the past few decades.[1] This is not to say that the distributive aspects of human population were not included in the writings of regional geographers in earlier periods. But it is only lately that population has become a main focus of work for a considerable group of the world's geographers. Indeed, at one time doubt was even expressed that man himself was an appropriate topic for geographic study. But such reticence has waned rapidly, and recently population geography has increased sharply in stature and productivity. In fact, some have even boldly contended that numbers, densities, and characteristics of human population provide the essential background for all geography.[2] Population serves as the point of reference from which all other geographic elements are observed, and from which they all, singly and collectively, derive significance and meaning.

In this book, where the paramount theme is population distribution patterns of world dimensions, both numbers and characteristics are involved. The first three chapters deal with numbers of humans. In Chapter 1, population numbers and their distributions over the earth's land surface are traced from prehistoric times to the beginning of the modern era. Emphasis is upon how the map of world population changed through several millenniums. Chapter 2 is concerned with the same theme, but focuses on the last three centuries, or the period since about 1650. Chapter 3 involves the contemporary scene. In Chapters 4 and 5 the theme of world patterns still prevails, but it is distribution of population characteristics, instead of numbers, that is in the forefront.

[1] Glenn T. Trewartha, "The Case for Population Geography," *Ann. Assoc. Am. Geographers*, Vol. 43, 1953, pp. 71–97.

[2] See D. J. M. Hoosen, "The Distribution of Population as the Essential Geographic Expression," *Can. Geographer*, Vol. 17, 1960, pp. 10–20.

Part 1

POPULATION NUMBERS:
WORLD DISTRIBUTION

Number of people is probably the most basic information about the earth and its regions. By comparison with population size, the number of tons of coal mined, of acres tilled, or the dollars of per capita national income earned, all are almost in the nature of embellishments. In a world whose basic organization is one of nation-states, it may be pointed out that population size is a major determinant of national power, for it largely resolves the size of both the labor force and the citizen military force. In addition, mass production and distribution are advantageously related to the magnitude of the population they serve.

3

CHAPTER
1

Population Distribution in the Past

THE PREHISTORIC AND EARLY HISTORIC PERIOD

The Food-Gathering and Hunting Stage. Ancient man of the genus Homo, using stone tools and fire, evolved on the earth at least half a million years ago. Homo sapiens, or modern man, characterized by a small chin and brow ridges and a high skull with flat sides, probably first appeared during the last interglacial period, 150,000 to 50,000 years back. Not only is the time of man's emergence blurred—the place of his beginnings is equally uncertain. It is likely, however, that the new species sprang from a number of different but related stocks which developed in several separate Old World tropical-subtropical centers. In all probability modern man evolved as a species and became differentiated into races somewhat simultaneously. Africa provided centers of major importance for human evolution and Asia furnished secondary ones,[1] with Europe more on the periphery than close to the centers of origin, and the Americas even more so.

From several Old World centers of origin, Paleolithic man, with his hunting and food-gathering economy, spread widely, although thinly and discontinuously, over much of the earth's land surface. By about 10,000 years ago, on the eve of the Agricultural Revolution, contemporaneous with the shrinking of the continental ice sheets in North America and Europe, human population may have sparsely and unevenly occupied Africa, Australia, much of Europe south of about 50°N, southwestern, southern, and parts of eastern Asia, and large parts of the Americas.[2]

Roughly 25,000 years ago, or before the arrival of humans in the Americas, the earth's total population may have been only 3.3 million;

---

[1] L. S. B. Leakey, The Origin of the Genus Homo. In Sol Tax (ed.), *Evolution after Darwin*, Vol. II: *The Evolution of Man.* University of Chicago Press, Chicago 1960. Pp. 18–19.

[2] Wm. W. Howells, "The Distribution of Man," *Scientific American,* Vol. 203, September 1960, figures on pp. 114–115.

15,000 years later it had expanded to possibly 5.3 million, so that the average density for the earth's land area is estimated to have been only 0.04 person per square kilometer (0.1 person per square mile).[3]

Although during the food-gathering stage a low level of population density prevailed everywhere, it was not the same at all times and all places. Thus, during the more "natural" food-collecting of full Pleistocene times the average population concentration is assumed to have been roughly 3.0 per 100 square miles; for the more specialized food gathering of late glacial and early postglacial times the estimate rises to 12.5 per 100 square miles.[4] These averages are derived from modern analogies of such regional variants as Caribou Eskimo, 1.07 per 100 square miles; Ojibwa wild rice gatherers, 13; Haida of the North American northwest coast, 247; Australian aborigines, 8.[5] Such density variations in peoples of the hunting and collecting stage were a consequence not so much of the average food potential as of food availability during the leanest season.[6]

As far as is known, except where there were unusually rich collecting grounds, Paleolithic man lived in small communities, probably varying from a half dozen to a dozen families. For such a group, operating from a single living center, an area the size of an American township (36 square miles) would be large enough to support the community in a reasonably plentiful environment.[7] There was no unnecessary moving about; a shifting of the community location occurred only when shortages made it necessary.

But in spite of the exceedingly small preagricultural population that occupied the earth at any one time, because of the extremely long duration of this period, a total of 66 billion hunters and gatherers may have walked the earth before men became plowmen and herdsmen.[8] This is more than half the total population that the earth has ever supported.

Agricultural Beginnings. The first significant acceleration in the growth trends of world population numbers came with the Agricultural Revolution, when man began to cultivate crops and domesticate animals,

---

[3] Edward S. Deevey, Jr., "The Human Population," *Scientific American*, Vol. 203, September 1960, pp. 196–197. See also Julian Huxley, "Population and Human Destiny," *Harpers*, Vol. 201, September 1950, pp. 38–46.

[4] Robert J. Braidwood and Charles A. Reed, "The Achievement and Early Consequences of Food Production: A Consideration of the Archeological and Natural-Historical Evidence," *Cold Spring Harbor Symposia on Quantitative Biology*, Vol. XXII, 1957, p. 21.

[5] Braidwood and Reed, "Food Production," p. 21 (data from Kroeber).

[6] Braidwood and Reed, "Food Production," p. 24.

[7] Carl O. Sauer, "Early Relations of Man to Plants," *Geog. Rev.*, Vol. 37, 1947, p. 20.

[8] Deevey, "Human Population," p. 197.

TABLE 1.1

Years Ago	Cultural Stage	Area Populated	Assumed Density Per Square Kilometer	Total Population (Millions)
1,000,000	Lower Paleolithic (hunting-gathering)	Africa	0.00425	0.125
300,000	Middle Paleolithic (hunting-gathering)	Africa and Eurasia	0.012	1
25,000	Upper Paleolithic (hunting-gathering)	Africa and Eurasia	0.04	3.34
10,000	Mesolithic (hunting-gathering)	All continents	0.04	5.32
6,000	Village farming and early urban	Old World New World	1.0 0.04	86.5
2,000	Village farming and urban	All continents	1.0	133
310 (1650)	Farming and industrial	All continents	3.7	545
210 (1750)	Farming and industrial	All continents	4.9	728
160 (1800)	Farming and industrial	All continents	6.2	906
60 (1900)	Farming and industrial	All continents	11.0	1,610
10 (1950)	Farming and industrial	All continents	16.4	2,400
A.D. 2000	Farming and industrial	All continents	46.0	6,270

SOURCE: Deevey, "Human Population."

starting in a few areas, subsequently spreading widely. The consequences were phenomenal. Limits on population within communities were gradually removed, and there no longer was the necessity for separation and spacing of living groups. Surpluses became available for exchange, and transport facilities between communities became essential. Isolation gave way to contact; change was more rapid. A greater abundance and an increased security of the food supply not only permitted more people to be supported per unit area, but in addition fewer people were required to produce the necessary food. As a consequence some were freed to concentrate on new activities, including the development of the non-agricultural crafts. It is not surprising, therefore, that weaving, the plow, the wheel, and metallurgy soon followed upon invention of agriculture.[9]

[9] Robert Braidwood, "The Agricultural Revolution," *Scientific American*, Vol. 203, September 1960, p. 148.

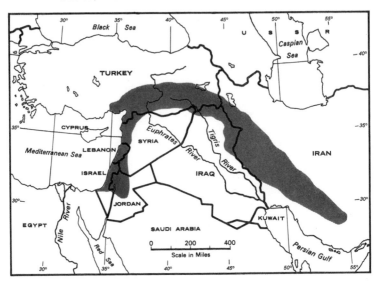

Figure 1.1. Hill lands flanking the Fertile Crescent, where the Agricultural Revolution began, are indicated by the shading.

The earliest beginnings of plant and animal domestication may have occurred some 8000 to 10,000 years ago among the inhabitants of the hill lands flanking the Fertile Crescent on the north, in modern Iraq and Iran (Fig. 1.1). Somewhat later there were similar developments in the Indian subcontinent and northern China, and still later in Central America, and possibly the Andes, and from these nuclear areas culture diffusion spread the new way of life to much the rest of the earth.

The archeological evidence indicates a population density of approximately 27 per square mile (about 10 per square kilometer) among the early village-farming peoples dwelling in the hill lands north of Mesopotamia some 8000 to 9000 years ago.[10] This average density of more than 2500 per 100 square miles for areas of village farming communities may be compared with estimates of average densities of 3 to 12.5 per 100 square miles for areas occupied by food-gathering peoples, or a differential amounting to several hundred times.[11] Thus as village farming spread more widely, the earth's population growth should have continued to accelerate, as it did. It was this change in food-acquiring techniques that caused the human population to increase much more over a period of a few thousand years than it had during the previous 250,000. Hence the earth's population, which is estimated to have been only

[10] Braidwood, "Agricultural Revolution," pp. 136–143.
[11] Braidwood and Reed, "Food Production," pp. 21–22.

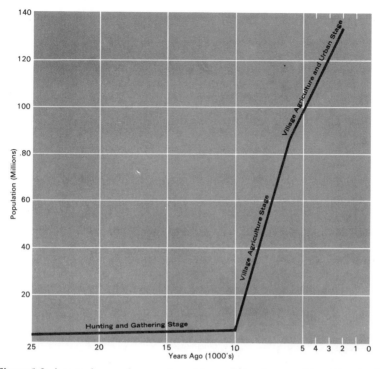

Figure 1.2. Assumed general rates of world population increase in prehistoric times. The slow rate of increase during the earlier hunting and gathering stage is to be contrasted with the more rapid growth rate during the village-agriculture stage associated with the Agricultural Revolution. (Data from Edward S. Deevey, Jr.)

about 5.3 .million some 10,000 years ago, may have swelled to nearly 16 times this figure—87 million—by 4000 years later.[12]

With the Agricultural Revolution, then, population moved up to a new plateau, both in magnitude and in density (Fig. 1.2). To be sure, not all of the earth's peoples graduated promptly from food gathering to agriculture; certainly most of the earth's surface, although not most of its population, continued in the gathering economy. About 5000 to 6000 years ago, on the eve of urban development, village agriculture had spread over most of nondesert western Asia and adjacent Mediterranean islands, southeastern Europe, the Mediterranean margins of Africa, the Indus Valley in India-Pakistan, parts of China, and some regions of Southeast Asia (Fig. 1.3). Recent archeological evidence indicates that some domestication of plants had now occurred in scattered spots in the Americas, notably the Tehuacan Valley in Mexico. But since more than

[12] Deevey, "Human Population," p. 196.

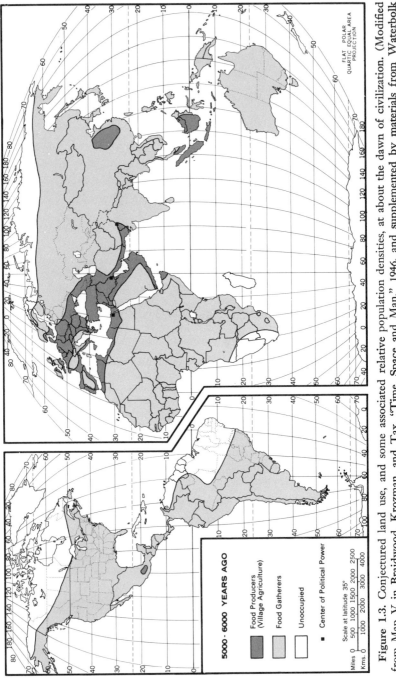
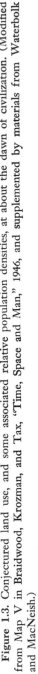

Figure 1.3. Conjectured land use, and some associated relative population densities, at about the dawn of civilization. (Modified from Map V in Braidwood, Krozman, and Tax, "Time, Space and Man," 1946, and supplemented by materials from Waterbolk and MacNeish.)

5000 - 6000 YEARS AGO

Food Producers
(Village Agriculture)

Food Gatherers

Unoccupied

■ Center of Political Power

Scale at latitude 35°
Miles 0 500 1000 1500 2000 2500
Kms. 0   1000   2000   3000   4000

FLAT   POLAR
QUARTIC EQUAL AREA
PROJECTION

70 percent of the region's food supply continued to come from wild plants and animals, there is little evidence to suggest a sudden increase in population.[13]

Thus, some five or six millenniums ago, the earth exhibited at least three distinct levels of population density:

1. The unoccupied lands, which probably included the northern margins of Eurasia and North America, parts of tropical South America, and dry southwestern Africa.
2. A thin scattering of preagricultural man over most of the remaining land area.
3. A degree of crowding much (perhaps scores or even hundreds of times) greater in those more restricted areas noted previously where village agriculture was intermingled with the gathering economy (Fig. 1.3).

Effects of City Development. The second great revolution in human culture, the rise of cities, with its associated piling up of population in restricted areas, denoted primarily a social change rather than a greater command of the natural environment such as accompanied the Agricultural Revolution. Approximately 5000 to 6000 years ago the beginnings of urban development appeared, first on the alluvial lands bordering the Tigris-Euphrates and Nile rivers, and somewhat later in the Indus Valley of Hindustan, and on the Hwang Delta of northern China. By 3500 years ago urbanism was relatively widespread in the eastern Mediterranean lands. Compared with the representative preurban agricultural village of 200–500 inhabitants which occupied only a few acres, the early dynastic cities of lower Mesopotamia, operating as centers for storage, exchange, and redistribution, spread over several hundred acres, and the largest contained several tens of thousands of people.[14]

There was no marked acceleration of world population growth coincident with urban development similar to that occurring with the beginnings of agriculture (Fig. 1.2). Agriculture continued to be the technical base for the earliest urban civilizations. There was no fundamental change of life-style, with its stimulation to population growth, accompanying early urbanization, comparable to that which followed upon the beginnings of agriculture. City dwellers continued to make up only a very small fraction of humanity. Indeed, world population remained overwhelmingly rural in all preindustrial societies. Still, those areas of most marked multiplication of towns and cities probably represented an overall greater density of population than did the exclusively

---

[13] Richard S. MacNeish, "Ancient Mesoamerican Civilization," *Science*, Vol. 143, Feb. 7, 1964, pp. 531–537.

[14] Robert M. Adams, "The Origin of Cities," *Scientific American*, Vol. 203, September 1960, p. 106. See also Robert J. Braidwood, "Near Eastern Prehistory," *Science*, Vol. 127, pp. 1419–1430.

agricultural areas. This is suggested by sample density figures for large tracts of inhabited country in parts of the Fertile Crescent as of about 4500 years ago: for village farmers like those at Jarmo in the Zagros hills, 2500 persons per 100 square miles; for urbanized Sumeria on the Mesopotamian Plain, 5000 per 100 square miles.[15] Although there are not enough data to arrive at a general ratio of local density for agricultural versus urbanized regions, the ratio of 1:2 determined from the preceding figures may give an idea of the situation.

It therefore seems fair to assume that a hypothetical population density map for the earth of about 3500 to 4000 years ago would show at least four general levels of concentration:

1. The unoccupied lands, chiefly in the northern parts of Eurasia and North America.
2. The areas of very low density where a gathering economy still prevailed, as it did in much of the Americas, tropical and southern Africa, the southern part of the conifer belt in Eurasia, and in Australia.
3. A markedly higher density in favored areas within those broadly dispersed regions of agricultural villages, which included the middle and low latitudes of Eurasia, spots within most of dry and subhumid northern Africa, and local areas in Latin America.
4. The highest level of average density in those regions combining cities and agricultural villages, as noted earlier (Fig. 1.4).

Great caution is required in deducing regional population densities from Figs. 1.3, 1.4, and 1.5 showing types of land use. The map legends have not been interrupted in regions of mountains and deserts. In such hostile environments, village agriculture with its higher densities was located in only a few favored spots.

By about 6000 years ago, the very early urban period, Deevey estimates the earth's population to have been around 86.5 million, with a density of about one person per square kilometer (2.7 per square mile) for the land areas in the Old World, and 0.04 person per square kilometer for those in the New World.[16]

THE ANCIENT-MEDIEVAL PERIOD (c. A.D. 0 to 1650)

The Ancient World. Around the beginning of the Christian Era the earth supported a population estimated at 133 to 300 million.[17] The very

[15] Braidwood and Reed, "Food Production," pp. 22–23.
[16] Deevey, "Human Population," pp. 196–197.
[17] Deevey, "Human Population," p. 196. See also *The Determinants and Consequences of Population Trends*, United Nations Population Study No. 17, New York, 1953, p. 8.

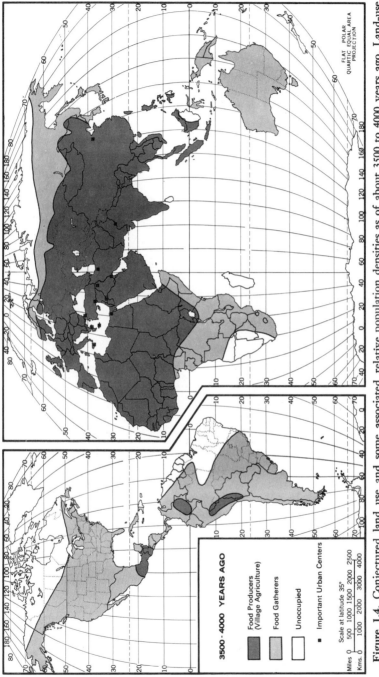
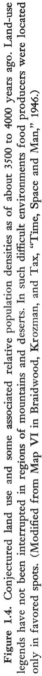

Figure 1.4. Conjectured land use and some associated relative population densities as of about 3500 to 4000 years ago. Land-use legends have not been interrupted in regions of mountains and deserts. In such difficult environments food producers were located only in favored spots. (Modified from Map VI in Braidwood, Krozman, and Tax, "Time, Space and Man," 1946.)

3500 - 4000 YEARS AGO

Food Producers
(Village Agriculture)

Food Gatherers

Unoccupied

■ Important Urban Centers

Scale at latitude 35°

Miles 0   500 1000 1500 2000 2500
Kms. 0 1000 2000 3000 4000

FLAT   POLAR
QUARTIC EQUAL AREA
PROJECTION

13

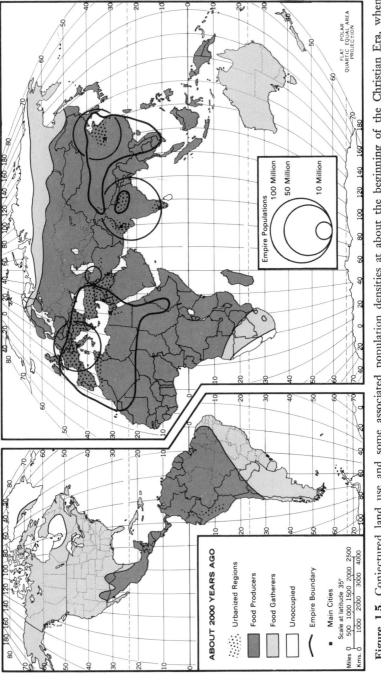

Figure 1.5. Conjectured land use and some associated population densities at about the beginning of the Christian Era, when great empires existed in the Mediterranean lands, East Asia, and probably in northern India. It should be cautioned that land-use legends have not been interrupted in regions of deserts and mountains. In such adverse environments food producers, with their higher population densities, were located in only a few favored spots. (Modified from Map VIII in Braidwood, Krozman, and Tax, "Time, Space and Man," 1946.)

ABOUT 2000 YEARS AGO

Urbanized Regions

Food Producers

Food Gatherers

Unoccupied

Empire Boundary

▪ Main Cities

Scale at latitude 35°

Miles 0 500 1000 1500 2000 2500
Kms. 0 1000 2000 3000 4000

Empire Populations

100 Million

50 Million

10 Million

FLAT POLAR QUARTIC EQUAL AREA PROJECTION

large range of the estimates suggests the fragmentary, unreliable, and indirect nature of the evidence on which they are based. It is nevertheless possible to outline some of the main features of population distribution as of about two millenniums back. Significantly, this Greco-Roman period was one characterized by great empires, with urban culture concentrated in three main centers of political power. In China the warring feudal states were unified by the Chin and Han dynasties. In India Asoka extended the Mauryan dominion throughout the northern plains and southward into the Deccan to beyond the 10°N parallel. The Mediterranean lands, and Europe farther north and west, came under Roman rule. Each of these empires was a focus of population containing probably many millions of people.

Perhaps the largest of these regions of concentration was in the Indian subcontinent where as of about the beginning of the second century B.C. Nath estimates population may have reached 100–140 million (Fig. 1.5).[18] A second and probably smaller center was located within present Mainland China where the Han census of A.D. 2 as interpreted by Bielenstein indicated a total of 57.7 million for the empire, which included some areas in what are now Manchuria, Korea, Mongolia, Turkestan, and Vietnam.[19] About 55 million were judged to be concentrated within the present boundaries of the 18 provinces of China proper, excluding Fukien, which at that time lay outside the empire. Employing the same census, but making what he believes are necessary adjustments, Durand arrives at a population of 71 million for China proper and 74 million for the empire.[20] Within Han China, probably three-quarters of the population was concentrated in the subhumid and semiarid north, mainly on the delta-plain of the Huang River (Fig. 1.6). Significantly, even as early as two millenniums ago, certain key features of the earth's present pattern of world population distribution were beginning to be discernible, for at that time at least one-half and possibly three-quarters of mankind may have been concentrated in two centers, one in southern and the other in eastern Asia.

The third concentration included the domain of the Roman Empire

[18] Pran Nath, *A Study of the Economic Conditions of Ancient India*, Royal Asiatic Society, London; 1929, Chap. 5. This estimate has been accepted by Davis as having reasonable validity. See Kingsley Davis, *The Population of India and Pakistan*, Princeton University Press, Princeton, N.J., 1951, p. 24.

[19] Hans Bielenstein, *The Census of China*, The Museum of Far Eastern Antiquities, Stockholm, Bull. No. 19, 1947, pp. 126–133.

[20] John D. Durand, "The Population Statistics of China, A.D. 2–1953." *Population Studies*, Vol. 13, 1960, p. 221. See also Albert Payson Usher, "The History of Population and Settlements in Eurasia," *Geog. Rev.*, Vol. 20, 1930, pp. 122–127.

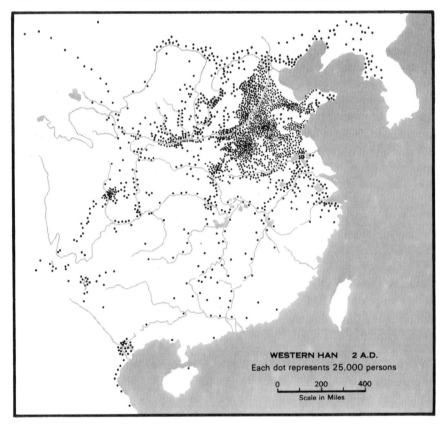

WESTERN HAN   2 A.D.
Each dot represents 25,000 persons

0   200   400
Scale in Miles

Figure 1.6. As of about the beginning of the Christian Era, population in China was strongly concentrated in the northern parts of the country, particularly on the delta-plain of the Huang, or Yellow, River. (After map by Hans Bielenstein, The Museum of Far Eastern Antiquities, Stockholm, Bull. No. 19, 1947.)

under Augustus, whose population Beloch estimates to have been about 54 million.[21] Russell is of the opinion that later studies, which suggest a modest upward revision of the preceding figure, have not greatly improved upon Beloch's work.[22] For centuries Rome surveyed the number of its citizens, but these counts are of little value in estimating Empire populations, for they omitted noncitizens as well as inhabitants of the provinces.[23] There was no serious interest in total population numbers,

[21] J. Beloch, *Die Bevölkerung der griechisch-römanischen Welt.* Duncker and Humbolt, Leipzig, 1886, p. 507.

[22] J. C. Russell, "Late Ancient and Medieval Populations," *Trans. Am. Phil. Soc.,* New Series, Vol. 48, Part 3, 1958, p. 7.

[23] Russell, "Ancient and Medieval Population," p. 6.

for there was no belief in the equality of individuals. Population counts of all heads are features mainly of democratic societies.

In the relatively dry lands of central and southwestern Asia (excluding the western portions of Asia bordering the Mediterranean and Black Seas, which were then parts of the Roman Empire) population was chiefly concentrated in the western parts. The whole of central Asia, with an area of 4,800,000 square kilometers, may have supported a total population of under 5 million.[24] Few estimates exist of numbers and distribution of people in the Middle East around the beginning of the Christian Era. The province of Syria, Russell conjectures, may have supported between 4 and 5 million inhabitants.[25] He also estimates the population of the whole Middle East as of about A.D. 600 at 18–19 million (Arabia, 1; Syria, 4; Mesopotamia, 9.1; the highlands, 4.6).[26] Thus the estimated population figures for Syria had not changed greatly from what they were more than half a millennium earlier, and perhaps the same can be assumed to apply to the rest of the Middle East. If so, it suggests that the population center of gravity was strongly oriented toward the western margins of the Middle East, with emphasis on Mesopotamia and Syria.

Following Beloch's regionalization of the Roman Empire's people, nearly 43 percent of the estimated 54 million resided in the European section, 36 percent in westernmost Asia, and a little more than 23 percent in North Africa. Population estimates for subdivisions of the three subcontinental parts of the Roman Empire previously noted, together with their densities, are shown in Table 1.2. Using Beloch's density data, except for revisions and some refinement in the cases of Italy and Greece, Usher has constructed a density map for the Roman Empire as of about the beginning of the Christian Era (Fig. 1.7).[27] The overall higher densities are observable in central Italy and the littoral of the eastern Mediterranean including western Asia and northern Africa. The Nile delta and floodplain of Egypt (465 per square mile) outstripped all other subdivisions in density of settlement, with parts of central Italy ranking next in order. Lowest densities were characteristic of Iberia, Gaul, and the Balkan Peninsula (Danube provinces).

The population of the Ancient Roman Empire, one-fifth to one-fourth of the earth's people, like the two Asian centers, was a forerunner of a much larger modern concentration of people—Europe. To be sure, the center of gravity of the European cluster underwent a westward and

[24] Russell, "Ancient and Medieval Populations," pp. 87–88.
[25] Russell, "Ancient and Medieval Populations," pp. 82–83.
[26] Russell, "Ancient and Medieval Populations," pp. 88–89.
[27] Usher, "Population and Settlement," p. 117.

northward shifting during the medieval and modern periods. Undoubtedly, however, the major lineaments of the earth's present pattern of population were beginning to take form as much as two millenniums back. Thus it appears that the three world population concentrations described previously might at that time together have nurtured 200 to 250 million people, certainly an overwhelming majority of all of mankind.

Little is known about the distribution of population outside of the three great empire concentrations. Thinly spread food-collecting peoples still occupied most of Anglo-America, the southern and southeastern

TABLE 1.2   Estimated Population of the Roman Empire at the
Death of Augustus, A.D. 14

	Population (in thousands)	Area (in thousands sq. km.)	Density	
			Per Sq. Km.	Per Sq. Mile
Total Roman Empire	54,000	3,340	16	41.5
1. European part	23,000	2,231	10	26
Italy	6,000	250	24	62.2
Sicily	600	26	23	59.5
Sardinia and Corsica	500	33	15	39
Narbonensis	1,500	100	15	39
Three Gauls	3,400	335	6.3	16.3
Danube	2,000	430	4.7	12.2
Greece	3,000	267	11	28.6
Spain	6,000	590	10	26
2. Asiatic part	19,500	665.5	30	77.5
Province of Asia	6,000	135	44	114
Rest of Asia Minor	7,000	413	17	44
Syria	6,000	109	55	143
Cyprus	500	9.5	52	135
3. African part	11,500	443	26	67.5
Egypt	5,000	28	179	465
Cyrenaica	500	15	33	85.5
Province of Africa	6,000	400	15	39

SOURCE: J. Beloch, *Griechisch-römanischen Welt*, p. 507.

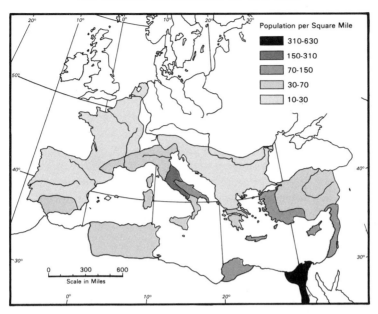

Figure 1.7. Population density in the Roman Empire at about the beginning of the Christian Era (death of Augustus, A.D. 14). (After map by A. P. Usher, *Geog. Rev.*, 1930.)

half of South America, southern Africa, Australia, and part of the coniferous-forest belt of northern Eurasia (Fig. 1.5). Agricultural populations with markedly higher densities spottily occupied large parts of tropical Latin America, most of Africa except the south, and all but northern Eurasia. Population densities of this time reached their maximum development within those regions of active empire building previously described, where urban development and long-distance trade were characteristic features of the economy.

The Medieval Period. The conjectures concerning the magnitude of the earth's population toward the close of the medieval and the beginning of the modern period (c. 1650) vary, with a median of about 500–600 million. This suggests roughly a twofold to threefold increase during the more than 1.5 millenniums since Augustus Caesar ruled the Roman Empire.[28] Such an inference points to a slow overall average growth rate of only 0.5 to 1.0 person per 1000 per year. But even this sluggish increase was erratic. It varied not only between regions, but also from one period to another within the same region, some parts even suffering absolute declines in periods of catastrophe.

[28] *Population Trends*, pp. 8–11. Deevey, "Human Population," p. 196.

Since the population figures suggested for this period are only sur-
mises, they are not very reliable for growth comparisons between
regions. From the weak evidence available, however, the East Asia
center, essentially China, is thought to have moved upward slowly but
erratically, so that it may have supported a total population of about
150 million by around 1600.[29] This could be double to triple what it
was at the advent of the Christian Era, indicating a rate of increase which
approximated that for the earth as a whole. The South Asian concentration in Hindustan, by contrast, is believed to have changed little over
the time span separating ancient from modern. Probably it experienced
periods of slow growth in more normal times, but inevitably catastrophes
in the form of famines, epidemics, and wars operated to wipe out previous gains. Thus the long-term trend in numbers showed a nearly
static condition.

The European center, resembling the East Asian more than that in
South Asia, probably experienced an emergent trend toward population
increase during the medieval period, but with strong general, and even
stronger regional fluctuations. Epidemics of the second to third, sixth,
and fourteenth centuries, the most devastating being that caused by the
bubonic plague, resulted in huge population losses in Europe and North
Africa. In the sixth and fourteenth centuries overall population declines
in the Europe-Asia Minor-North Africa center may have amounted to
40 percent (see Table 1.3).[30] For the Middle Ages as a whole there was
a pronounced increase of population in the frontier regions lying to the
north of the Alps and Carpathians, as the forest lands were cleared and
occupied by agricultural peoples. Thus Germany grew from 2 or 3
million in Caesar's time to 17 million early in the seventeenth century.
Likewise the Slavic nations of east-central Europe multiplied in population numbers from an estimated 8.5 million at about A.D. 1000 to about
18 million in the early 1700s.[31] Southern and western Europe and the
Mediterranean lands of western Asia and northern Africa grew less
rapidly and there were important regional fluctuations. Actual declines
took place in the Greek states, Spain, and Italy.

The Earth's Population Pattern as of about 1650. Assuming the
estimates are reasonably correct and the earth actually did support some
500 to 600 million people at the beginning of the modern period, or
double to triple what it did at the time of Augustus Caesar, how were

[29] Ping-ti Ho. *Studies on the Population of China, 1368–1953.* Harvard University
Press, Cambridge, Mass., 1959, p. 264.

[30] Russell, "Ancient and Medieval Populations," pp. 40–45.

[31] *Population Trends,* pp. 9–10.

TABLE 1.3   Population Estimates (In Millions) At Specified Times

Area	A.D.1	350	600 [a]	800	1000	1200	1340	1400	1500
Greece	3	2	1.2	2	5	4	2	—	1.5
Balkans	2	3	1.8	3	—	—	2	—	3
Asia Minor	8.8	11.6	7	8	8	7	8	—	6
Syria	4.4	4.4	4	4	2	2.7	3	—	2
Egypt	4.5	3	2.7	3	3	2	3	—	2.5
North Africa	4.2	2	1.8	1	1	1.5	2	—	3.5
Iberia	6	4	3.6	4	7	8	9.5	—	8.3
Gaul	6.6	5	3	5	—	—	—	—	—
France and the Low Countries	—	—	—	—	6	10	19	—	16
Italy	7.4	4	2.4	4	5	7.8	9.3	—	5.5
Germany	3.5	3.5	2.1	4	4	7	11	—	7
Scandinavia	—	—	—	—	—	—	–.6	—	–.5
British Isles	0.4	0.3	0.8	1.2	1.7	2.8	5.3	—	4
Slavia	4	4.8	2.8	6	—	—	—	—	—
Poland, etc.	—	—	—	—	1	1.2	1.2	—	2
Russia	—	—	—	—	7.5	6	8	—	6
Hungary	—	—	—	—	1	2	2	—	2
Totals	54.8	47.6	33.2	45.2	52.2	61	85.9	52 [b]	70.8

SOURCE: Russell, "Ancient and Medieval Populations," 148.
[a] Reductions in population for plague of sixth century: general, 40 percent; Syria, Egypt, Spain and North Africa, 10 percent.
[b] Total reduced 40 percent from that of 1340.

the additional 200–300 million distributed, and how did the world map of population in 1650 differ substantially from that of the first century? While the unreliable nature of the population estimates precludes any precise measurement of change, it may be warranted to set forth some probable crude features of population redistribution.

If it is assumed that Asia in the first and second centuries had a population of about 175–200 million, including more than 20 million in western Asia, it may be inferred that 100 million or more were added in eastern and southern Asia during the millennium and a half comprising the late ancient and medieval periods. This suggests that as of about 1650, 50–60 percent of the earth's population was concentrated in eastern and southern Asia, a proportion close to the current one and probably not much less than its proportion in the first century. The early concentration of the earth's population in eastern and southern Asia and the en-

TABLE 1.4 Estimates of World Population by Regions as of about 1650 (in millions)

World	545
Africa	100
Northern America	1
Latin America	12
Asia (excluding U.S.S.R.)	327
Europe and Asiatic U.S.S.R.	103
Oceania	2

SOURCE: Original estimates by A. M. Carr-Saunders, *World Population*, Chap. 14. as modified in *Population Trends*, p. 11.

during character of this concentration through two millenniums of time, is one of the primary features of the earth's population geography.

There were also some important redistributions of population within Asia. Of the possible 100 million or more added in the general region of East and South Asia, the greatest increment was probably in China, where population rose from an estimated total of 60–70 million in about A.D. 1 to 150 million in 1600.[32] Taeuber estimates that there were at this time in the neighborhood of 20 million inhabitants in Japan and modest additions must be credited to Ceylon and Southeast Asia. With no information to the contrary, it is assumed that the Indian subcontinent had not changed greatly in population since the time of Augustus Caesar (Fig. 1.8).[33] It was eastern Asia, therefore, that probably experienced the greatest growth.

Africa as of around 1650 is conjectured by Carr-Saunders to have supported a total population of about 100 million. Beloch inferred that the whole of the north African part of the Roman Empire may have contained 11.5 million inhabitants at the time of Augustus, but nothing is said about the continent as a whole. Since Mediterranean Africa probably contained fewer people in the sixteenth and seventeenth centuries than it did a millennium and a half earlier, it seems that over 90 million were concentrated in the humid tropical lands south of the Sahara.[34] But what their distribution may have been is unknown.

[32] Ho, *Population of China*, p. 264.
[33] Davis, *India and Pakistan*, p. 24.
[34] Russell, "Ancient and Medieval Populations," pp. 130–131; 148.

Other than Asia and Africa, which may account for roughly a 200-million population increase, or perhaps two-thirds of the total population increment for the whole earth between the first century and 1650, most of the remaining increase was probably in Europe, a center that already had been fairly conspicuous at the beginning of the Christian Era. Beloch credited the Roman Empire of that time with a total of 54

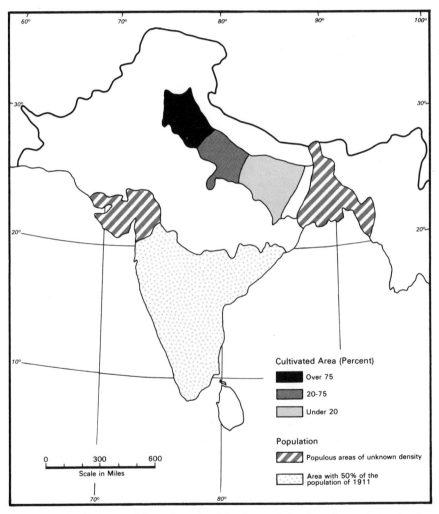

Figure 1.8. Conjectured intensity of cultivation and density of population in the Indian Subcontinent in about 1600 A.D. compared with conditions there in the twentieth century. (After map by A. P. Usher, *Geog. Rev.*, 1930.)

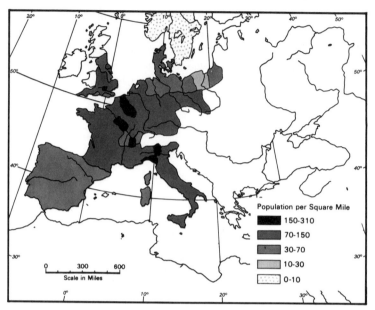

Figure 1.9. Population densities in western Europe in about 1700. (After map by A. P. Usher, *Geog. Rev.*, 1930.)

million, of which the European part had 23 million. If the Carr-Saunder's figure of about 100 million for Europe in 1650 has some validity, then Europe may have added close to 75 million people over the medieval period. Again, insufficient statistical evidence permits no precise allocation of this increment and the consequent redistribution of people (Figs. 1.9, 1.10). Some absolute gain was probably experienced in southern Europe in those long-settled areas which had been a part of the old Roman Empire. Thus Italy may have grown from 6 to 13 million, Iberia from 6 to 10, and France from 6 or 7 to 16 million.[35] As noted earlier, however, the maximum gains in population were experienced in the more newly settled lands of northwestern, central, and eastern Europe, now Britain, the Low Countries, Germany, Scandinavia, Poland, Hungary, Czechoslovakia, and Russia. Probably half or more of the European population in 1650 was outside those parts of the continent not tributary to the Mediterranean Sea.

Controversy prevails concerning what contribution the Western Hemisphere made to the earth's total population as of the beginning of the modern era. Most modern scholars have been very conservative in their estimates. Kroeber, for example, surmised only 8,400,000 in-

[35] Earlier figures from Beloch; later ones from Russell.

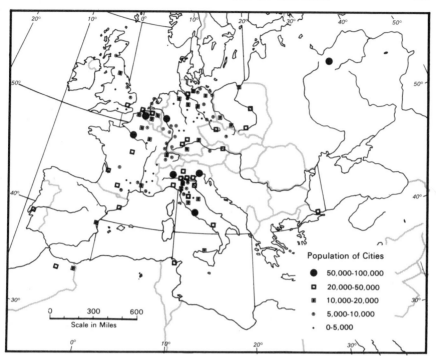

Figure 1.10. Urban population in Europe in the late medieval period. (*Source:* J. C. Russell, "Late Ancient and Medieval Populations," *Trans. Am. Phil. Soc.*, Vol. 58, 1968.)

habitants for the entire New World in 1500.[36] By contrast, the most recent estimates have been much higher, with Woodrow Borah suggesting 100 million and Henry Dobyns 90 million.[37] But even if these latest, larger estimates of pre-Columbian native population in the New World are accepted, authorities seem to agree there was catastrophic decline, estimated at 90–95 percent, in many regions during the first 100 years or so after initial contact with Europeans.[38] A major cause for this

[36] A. L. Kroeber, *Cultural and Natural Areas of Native North America.* University of California Publications in American Archaeology and Ethnology No. 38, Berkeley, 1939, p. 166.

[37] Woodrow Borah, "America as Model: The Demographic Impact of European Expansion upon the Non-European World," *Actas y Memorias, XXXV Congreso Internacional de Americanistas*, Mexico, 1964, Vol. 3, pp. 379–387, esp. p. 381. H. F. Dobyns, "Estimating Aboriginal American Population: An Appraisal of Techniques with a New Hemispheric Estimate," *Current Anthropology*, Vol. 7, 1966, pp. 395–416, esp. p. 415.

[38] Borah, "America as Model," fn. 2, p. 382, Dobyns, "Aboriginal American Populations," fn. 2, pp. 413–415.

decimation of the aboriginal population was the epidemics of newly introduced Old World diseases, for which the natives had no immunity. Thus by about 1650 population in the New World may have been sparse indeed. It does not seem so unusual, therefore, that Durand's "low" and "high" variants of population estimates for the Americas for 1750 are only 14 and 23 million. Of these, Anglo-America may have contributed 2–3 million and Latin America 12–20 million.[39] Dobyns estimates the aboriginal population of Latin America at its nadir, around 1650, to have been only about 4,000,000.[40]

The pre-Columbian centers of most advanced culture, and presumably also the largest populations, were in highland Mexico, the Maya settlement area in Central America, and the Inca region of the central Andes in Peru and northernmost Bolivia.

On a world map of population density as of the seventeenth century, the known areas of population concentration, and therefore high relative density, were to be found in northern and eastern China and southern Japan, concentrated largely in the alluvial lowlands; in the Indian subcontinent, with the greatest crowding probably in the northern and southern extremities; and Mediterranean, western, and central Europe. Smaller units of high relative density were centered in Mediterranean Africa, especially the Nile Valley; Mediterranean Asia; and Mesopotamia.[41] There were a few small centers in Latin America, mainly in Mexico, Central America, and the Peruvian-Bolivian Andes.

REFERENCES

Adams, Robert M. "The Origin of Cities," *Scientific American*, Vol. 203, September 1960, pp. 153–168.

Beloch, J. *Die Bevölkerung der griechisch-römanischen Welt.* Duncker and Humbolt, Leipzig, 1886.

Borah, Woodrow. "America as Model: The Demographic Impact of European Expansion upon the Non-European World," *Actas y Memorias, XXXV Congreso Internacional de Americanistas.* Mexico, 1964. Vol. 3, pp. 379–387.

Braidwood, Robert. "The Agricultural Revolution," *Scientific American,* Vol. 203, September 1960, pp. 131–148.

Carr-Saunders, A. M. *World Population: Past Growth and Present Trends.* Clarendon, Oxford, 1936.

[39] John S. Durand, "The Modern Expansion of World Population," *Population Problems, Proc. Am. Phil. Soc.,* Vol. III, No. 3, June 1967, p. 138.

[40] Dobyns, "Aboriginal American Populations," p. 415.

[41] Usher, "Population and Settlement," pp. 120, 126, 130, 131.

Childe, V. G. *What Happened in History*. Penguin, London, 1942.

Cipolla, Carlo M. *The Economic History of World Population*. Pelican Books, Baltimore, Md. (A 537); Penguin Books, Harmondsworth, 1962.

Clark, Colin. *Population Growth and Land Use*. Macmillan, London, 1967. Chap. 3, pp. 59–122.

Davis, Kingsley. *The Population of India and Pakistan*. Princeton University Press, Princeton, N.J., 1951.

Deevey, Edward S., Jr. "The Human Population," *Scientific American*, Vol. 203, September 1960, pp. 195–204.

Dobyns, H. F. "Estimating American Aboriginal Population: An Appraisal of Techniques with a New Hemispheric Estimate," *Current Anthropology*, Vol. 7, 1966, pp. 395–416.

Durand, J. D. World Population Estimates, 1750–2000. Paper contributed to the United Nations World Population Conference, Belgrade, 1965, Vol. II, p. 17. United Nations Document E/CONF.41/3.

Howells, Wm. W. "The Distribution of Man," *Scientific American*, Vol. 203, September 1960, pp. 113–127.

Huxley, Julian. "Population and Human Density," *Harpers Magazine*, September 1950, pp. 32–46.

Kroeber, A. L. *Anthropology*. Harcourt, Brace, New York, 1948.

Moreland, W. H. *India at the Death of Akbar*. Macmillan, London, 1920.

Nath, Pran. *A Study of the Economic Conditions of Ancient India*. Royal Asiatic Society, London, 1929. Chap. 5.

Ohlin, Goran. Historical Outline of World Population Growth. Paper prepared for the United Nations World Population Conference, Belgrade, 1965.

Reinhard, M., and A. Armengaud. *Histoire generale de la population mondiale*. Editions Montchrestien, Paris, 1961.

Russell, J. C. "Late Ancient and Medieval Populations," *Trans. Am. Phil. Soc.*, New Series, Vol. 48, 1958.

United Nations Population Study No. 17. *The Determinants and Consequences of Population Trends*. New York, 1953. Pp. 5–10.

Usher, Abbott Payson. "The History of Population and Settlement in Eurasia," *Geog. Rev.*, Vol. 20, 1930, pp. 110–132. (Maps)

Waterbolk, H. T. "Food Production in Prehistoric Europe," *Science*, December 6, 1968, pp. 1093–1102.

CHAPTER

2

The Modern Period (after c. 1650)

An assumed population base of about 470–545 million in the mid-1600s grew to slightly more than 2500 million (estimated) by 1950 (2998 by 1960, and 3551 by early 1969). Some of the most noteworthy events in world population growth and redistribution have occurred during the last three centuries, rivaling in importance even those stemming from the Agricultural Revolution some 7 to 9 millenniums back.

ACCELERATED POPULATION GROWTH

As had the Agricultural Revolution in an earlier time, in the modern period the Industrial-Scientific Revolution led to an amazingly accelerated rate of population increase. Not only did numbers soar, but according to most estimates, they soared at an even increasing rate (Fig. 2.1). The "medium" estimates [1] suggest an approximate fivefold multiplication of human population over the three centuries 1650–1950, and roughly a six-times increase to 1960. This is an average annual increase of around 5 or 6 per 1000 (0.5 to 0.6 percent). Such a rate of increase may not appear rapid compared with the present annual rate of probably 20 per 1000, or 2 percent. Yet it is 5 to 10 times greater than the average growth rate during the much longer span of years from ancient to modern times. Moreover, within the modern period itself the growth rate seems to be inexorably upward: 1650–1750, perhaps 3–4 per 1000; 1750–1800, 4; 1800–1850, 5; 1850–1900, 5–6; and 1900–1950, 8. In the most recent *decade*, 1950–1960, the growth rate was 18.

Two phases of modern world population trend seem to be obvious.

[1] The population estimates used for periods prior to 1900 are "medium" estimates, and many of the growth rates would be changed considerably by selecting different plausible variants for regions and dates. An accelerated growth seems acceptable for a majority of the earth's regions; the opposite is true of the estimates for China.

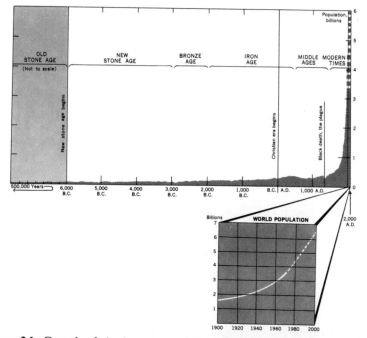

Figure 2.1. Growth of the human population. Note the remarkable acceleration over the past two centuries. It has taken hundreds of thousands of years for man to reach his 1960 numbers of about three billion. But in some 40 more years, or roughly the year 2000, the earth's population will probably grow to six or seven billion. (Modified from diagrams in *Population Bulletin*, February, 1962. From Elements of Geography, by Trewartha, Robinson and Hammond. McGraw-Hill.)

From about 1750 to 1900 growth was at a relatively moderate speed (but still much more rapid than those of premodern epochs), while between 1900 and 1950 there was a sharp acceleration in rate of growth (Fig. 2.2). In the earlier phase the rate was probably about 4–5 per 1000 per year; it almost doubled in the period 1900–1950, and there was another impressive jump in the 1950s and 1960s. Estimates suggest that before the modern era (up to the close of the Middle Ages) population doubled in periods fluctuating between 1000 and 2000 years. In the eighteenth century the doubling period dropped to under 200 years, in the nineteenth century to roughly 100 years. Still another method of indicating the acceleration of population growth is by the varying time spans required for each increase of one billion, using the median variant projection of population growth.[2]

[2] Jean Bourgeois-Pichat, *Population Growth and Development*, International Conciliation, Carnegie Endowment for International Peace, January 1966, No. 556, p. 8.

TABLE 2.1 Estimates of World Population by Regions, 1650–2000

		Estimated Population (in millions)						
	World Total	Africa	Northern America	Latin America	Asia (exc. U.S.S.R.)	Europe and U.S.S.R.	Oceania	Area of European Settlement
Willcox's estimate, 1650 [a]	470	100	1	7	257	103	2	113
Carr-Saunder's estimate, 1650 [b]	545	100	1	12	327	103	2	118
Durand's "medium" estimates [c]								
1750	791	106	2	16	498	167	2	—
1800	978	107	7	24	630	208	2	—
1850	1,262	111	26	38	801	284	2	—
1900	1,650	133	82	74	925	430	6	—
United Nation's estimate [d]								
1920	1,860	143	116	90	1,023	482	8.5	696
1930	2,069	164	134	107	1,120	534	10	786
1940	2,295	191	144	130	1,244	575	11.1	860
1950	2,515	222	166	162	1,381	572	12.7	914
1960	2,998	273	199	212	1,659	639	15.7	1,066
Durand's estimate, 2000 [c]	6,130	768	354	638	3,458	880	32	—

NOTE: "Median" estimates used throughout this table represent the center of a range of plausible figures for each area and date.

[a] Willcox, American Demography.
[b] Carr-Saunders, World Population.
[c] Durand, "Expansion of World Population."
[d] U.N., World Population Prospects, 1966.

1810	1st billion	several hundred thousand years
1925	2nd billion	115 years
1960	3rd billion	35 years
1980	4th billion	20 years
1993	5th billion	13 years

TABLE 2.2   Estimates of World Population Growth, 1650–2000 (annual rate of increase per 1000, since preceding date)

Period	World	More Developed Areas	Less Developed Areas
1650–1750	4	—	—
1750–1800	4	—	—
1800–1850	5	—	—
1850–1900	5	—	—
1900–1950	8	—	—
1900–1920	6	—	—
1920–1930	11	12	11
1930–1940	10	8	13
1940–1950	10	3	13
1950–1960	18	14	21
1950–2000	18	10	20

SOURCES: Durand, "Expansion of World Population," p. 140; U.N., *World Population Prospects*, 1966; Willcox, *American Demography*.

On the basis of the 1960 growth rate, the earth's population will reach 135.8 billion by the year 2220, or about one person per square meter of land surface—certainly a catastrophic situation for humanity. The present growth rate of about 20 per 1000, an all-time high, portends a doubling of the earth's population within about 35 years, or an eightfold increase within a century. The increment in world population since 1900 approximates the planet's total population in 1900—only two-thirds of a century ago. Progressive acceleration in population growth, with all its attendant effects, many of them adverse, is a distinguishing feature of the modern era. This quickening of growth relates to the

TABLE 2.3 "Medium" Estimates of Population of the World and Major Areas, 1750–1950, and Projections to 2000

Areas	Population (millions)						Annual Rate of Increase (percent)				
	1750	1800	1850	1900	1950	2000	1750–1800	1800–1850	1850–1900	1900–1950	1950–2000
World total	791	978	1,262	1,650	2,515	6,130	0.4	0.5	0.5	0.8	1.8
Asia (exc. U.S.S.R.)	498	630	801	925	1,381	3,458	0.5	0.5	0.3	0.8	1.9
China (Mainland)	200	323	430	436	560	1,034	1.0	0.6	0.0	0.5	1.2
Indian and Pakistan	190	195	233	285	434	1,269	0.1	0.3	0.4	0.8	2.2
Japan	30	30	31	44	83	122	0.0	0.1	0.7	1.3	0.8
Indonesia	12	13	23	42	77	250 [a]	0.2	1.2	1.2	1.2	2.4
Remainder of Asia (exc. U.S.S.R.)	67	69	87	118	227	783	0.1	0.5	0.7	1.3	2.5
Africa	106	107	111	133	222	768	0.0	0.1	0.4	1.0	2.5
North Africa	10	11	15	27	53	192	0.2	0.5	1.2	1.4	2.8
Remainder of Africa	96	96	96	106	169	576	0.0	0.0	0.2	0.9	2.5
Europe (exc. U.S.S.R.)	125	152	208	296	392	527	0.4	0.6	0.7	0.6	0.6
U.S.S.R.	42	56	76	134	180	353	0.6	0.6	1.1	0.6	1.4
America	18	31	64	156	328	992	1.1	1.5	1.8	1.5	2.2
Northern America	2	7	26	82	166	354	–	2.7	2.3	1.4	1.5
Middle and South America	16	24	38	74	162	638	0.8	0.9	1.3	1.6	2.8
Oceania	2	2	2	6	13	32	–	–	–	1.6	1.8

SOURCE: Durand, "Expansion of World Population," p. 137.
[a] Calculated by assuming that Indonesia's share in the projected total for Southeast Asia would be the same in 2000 as in 1980.

TABLE 2.4 Estimates of World Population Growth, 1900–1960

Date	Population (millions)	Annual Rate of Increase since Preceding Date (percent)
1900	1,650	—
1920	1,860	0.6
1930	2,069	1.1
1940	2,295	1.0
1950	2,515	1.0
1960	2,998	1.8

SOURCE: Durand, "Expansion of World Population," p. 140.

modernization that was in progress for a large segment of the earth's inhabitants, which in turn initiated the demographic transition.[3]

The relatively simultaneous upturn of the population trend in the eighteenth and early nineteenth centuries in widely separated and diverse regions of the earth is a puzzle not yet solved. There seems to have been some still unidentified common causal factor. Durand questions whether it may not be related to the worldwide epidemiological, as well as economic, repercussions of the European voyages of discovery and conquest during and after the fifteenth century.[4]

One writer has compared the growth of the earth's population to a long, thin powder fuse that burns slowly and haltingly until it finally reaches the charge and then explodes. Throughout 99 percent of human history, population remained sparse and grew slowly. The first real burst in population growth—the explosion at the end of the fuse—came with the latest epoch in human progress: the Scientific-Industrial Revolution. This involved not merely technological advances but associated economic, social, and political changes as well. Three centuries ago the world had what, by present rates of growth, appears to have been almost a stationary population. This was the result of a high death rate nearly canceling out the effects of a high birth rate. Probably half the children died before reaching the age of 10; 50 percent of the population was under 20; old people were few; the waste of life was colossal.

[3] The term "demographic transition," to be elaborated later in the chapter, refers to the succession of changes in birth, death, and natural increase rates that accompanies the process of a country's modernization.

[4] John D. Durand, "The Modern Expansion of World Population," *Proc. Am. Phil. Soc.*, Vol. III, No. 3, 1967, p. 142

Considering the world as a whole, this recent explosive growth of population must be viewed with great concern. But, oddly, this concern has been manifested mainly during the last decade or two only. Actually the problems posed by world population growth are both long-run and short-run, the two often being confused. In the long run, of course, equilibrium must be reached between birth rates and death rates. This is the problem of the balance of nature characteristic of all living things. But this long-term problem probably should not be invoked to indicate the present urgent necessity for birth control. Such control is chiefly justified by the short-run problem that burgeoning population growth in the less developed countries is threatening their economic growth and the improvement of their populations' well-being, and thereby endangering the peace of the world.

On an earth where equality of production and consumption prevailed, population could multiply several times without anyone suffering a serious food deficiency. But as the world is now, there are numerous national and regional populations where food deficiencies already prevail, and in many of these, population increase will seriously aggravate the economic situation. Indeed the prevailing expert opinion has been heavily weighted toward the belief that world food production, especially in the already crowded less developed countries, was lagging behind the burgeoning population. The anticipated result of this bleak outlook was large-scale regional famine in the not-too-distant future. But in recent months, certain U.S. Department of Agriculture officials have voiced more optimistic opinions concerning the future food supply. The optimism seems to have been inspired in part by the phenomenal successes obtained in the development of new high-yielding varieties of food grains, and by the increased production of wheat and rice in India, Pakistan, and the Philippines. Such disagreement among the experts can only leave the layman confused. But if the current highly promising agricultural changes are to yield large-scale results in the less developed realm, they must be accompanied there by widespread technological, economic, and social change, and since such changes come slowly, it would seem unwise to expect a quick relief from present hunger and the threat of future famine in large parts of the world's traditional societies.

No doubt in wealthier and more advanced countries the output of food and goods can stay ahead of increasing population for some time to come. In some of these, high population densities are less an objective fact of economics and living standards and more a subjective feeling of suffocation and surfeit with mass humanity. Biologists have discovered that among some lower animals, when crowding reaches a certain level, physical deterioration, especially of the nervous system, results. The animals become more susceptible to a variety of maladies, but they suffer particularly from what may be called "shock disease." There is a possibility that humans subjected to crowding may similarly suffer. Indeed, the widespread use of tranquilizer drugs may be indicative of a kind of "shock disease." It is especially in the affluent societies, equipped as they are with the power and technology to modify their surroundings, that environmental deterioration has become serious, so that there has come to be a shrinking and spoiling of the beautiful and of esthetic values. Rivers and lakes are befouled, the air is polluted, wilderness areas shrink, access to beaches diminishes, and all the amenities dependent on land and space become more and more scarce, while shabbiness expands. Clearly then there is no such thing as a *world* population problem. Different parts of the world, and even different countries, pose different problems for which there is no common solution.

Although the earth's regional population problems are scarcely new, it is only very recently that the gravity of the total situation, especially as it applies to the less developed realm, has penetrated world consciousness enough so that remedial programs have been seriously considered. At last the idea seems to be taking hold that by some humane method—and not a return to high death rates—the proliferation of human life must be controlled.

The Scientific-Industrial Revolution. The Scientific-Industrial Revolution, which led to so many significant population changes, began in western Europe, spread quickly to areas of European settlement overseas and then only partially and much more slowly to non-Western cultures. The term Industrial Revolution is imprecise, for that event neither occurred at the same time in different countries, nor were its overlapping and interrelated elements similar in all regions affected. The chief danger lies in interpreting the Industrial Revolution too narrowly and viewing it mainly as the inception and growth of factory industry. Admittedly the transformation was greater in manufacturing than in other economic sectors, but agriculture, mining, transportation, and construction all were retooled as well. In its later stages it has been even more a scientific than an industrial revolution, involving among other things public sanitation, scientific medicine, electronics, automation, and most recently the development and application of computer systems. It is to this Scientific Revolution and its impact upon medicine, pharmacy, and sanitation that the rapid steepening of the population growth curve since about 1900 is due.

The direct economic impact of all the new machines and technological processes was tremendous, but equally dramatic were the changes induced in the social structure. These involved not only farm people, but even more the factory workers and entrepreneurs who came to be highly concentrated in the rapidly multiplying and expanding towns and cities.

All aspects of change were not simultaneous and the order of their occurrence was not everywhere the same. In England, where the Industrial Revolution began earliest (about 1750), within a period of 80 to 100 years the nation's economy and social structure underwent complete transformation. The earlier three-field agriculture involving village settlements and common fields was supplanted by enclosed fields, individual ownership, markedly improved husbandry, and, of course, increased output. Some of these changes had begun even as early as the late seventeenth century. The processing of goods, which previously had been scattered in homes and workshops throughout the countryside, became increasingly concentrated in larger factories within new urban centers. Isolation of the countryside came to an end as roads and canals multiplied and men and goods moved easily. Later transportation improvements—steamships and steam locomotives—further stimulated commerce and industry. In this way commercial agriculture had its beginnings. Expanding ocean transport carried the developing agricultural techniques of Europe to new and fertile lands overseas, whose surpluses shortly began to stream back to Europe. Significantly, each improvement in one sector stimulated all others, creating a snowballing effect which was revolutionary in its rapidity and scope. It remains to be pointed out how these economic and social changes influenced population growth.

Two factors alone—fertility and mortality—determine the number of people for the earth as a whole. But in the early modern period, or prior to about 1850, the meager and fragmentary nature of the evidence makes it difficult to determine whether it was declining mortality or rising fertility, or perhaps both, that produced the accelerated growth of world population. The standard typology of the demographic transition indicates that a decline in mortality normally initiates the upward trend in growth rates in modernizing societies. But the assumed decline in deaths is itself a puzzle, and one difficult to verify from available statistics, or to relate with assurance to known institutional changes. Very likely, the appreciably accelerated growth rate before the mid-1800s was a consequence of both a decline in mortality and a rise in fertility. For most modern Western cultures there probably took place a rise in birth rates before the normal long-continued decline set in.[5] Admittedly this idea is not in harmony with the model of the demo-

[5] William Petersen, *Population*, Macmillan, New York, 1961, p. 401.

graphic transition usually set forth, which posits a declining death rate as the sole cause of the upward trend in population growth in the early stages of modernizing Western societies. Although a rise in fertility in early nineteenth-century Europe cannot be adequately documented, reasons for its possible occurrence in the early modern period may be related to the dissolution of rural village society and the weakening of the ethical and institutional patterns which village living promoted. In the process of dissolution, increased births may have resulted from both more marriages and lower age of marriage, a less effective control of conception by married couples, and a higher rate of illegitimacy.[6] The simultaneous falling mortality may in part be related to an improved agriculture, which provided a more abundant and varied food supply. As diets improved there probably came to be a lower incidence of food-deficiency diseases. Contributing also may have been a slow improvement of living conditions in general as factories began to provide a larger and more inexpensive supply of consumer goods. More effective winter heating of residences and places of work conceivably improved the public health.

The accelerated growth after the mid-1800s is almost exclusively a result of the more consistent and rapid fall in the death rate in European societies. No longer were rising birth rates a factor, as they probably had been in the earlier periods. Better health and lower mortality may be attributed to several causes—greater attention to purification of public water supplies and to effective sewage and garbage disposal, especially in urban areas; improved habits of personal hygiene; increased cleanliness, including more frequent bathing and greater availability and use of soap; the later nineteenth-century development of aseptics and antiseptics for the exclusion or killing of pathogenic organisms; and artificial immunization against various diseases through the development of vaccines.[7]

As mentioned earlier, an initial period of likely increased births among at least some modernizing Western nations preceded a long period of general fertility decline as society became progressively more industrial and urban. Why births became fewer in the new urban environment is not fully understood. It seems to be agreed, though, that the cause was cultural, not physical. There was no impairment in the physical ability of urban women to bear children. Rather, the new cultural setting seems to have engendered a desire for smaller families, and also the means to accomplish it. Numerous children were useful on a farm, much less so

---

[6] Petersen, *Population*, pp. 396–400.

[7] Ralph Thomlinson, *Population Dynamics*, Random House, New York, 1965, pp. 91–94.

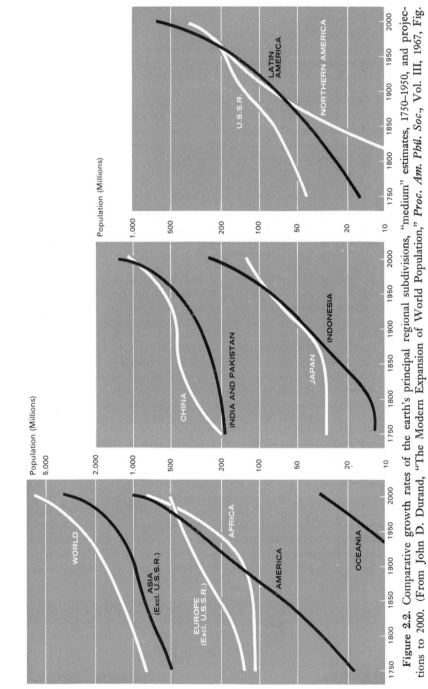

Figure 2.2. Comparative growth rates of the earth's principal regional subdivisions, "medium" estimates, 1750–1950, and projections to 2000. (From John D. Durand, "The Modern Expansion of World Population," *Proc. Am. Phil. Soc.*, Vol. III, 1967, Fig. 12.)

in a city. Indeed, they were often more burden than asset. Moreover, they were a greater expense to educate, feed, and clothe in the urban environment. Also, as families became more mobile, large families became less desirable.

REGIONAL DIFFERENTIAL RATES OF GROWTH

A second population feature of the modern period, in addition to accelerated overall growth rates, is that these rates show striking differences among peoples and among regions (Fig. 2.2). Such differentials had important economic and political consequences, which in turn resulted in large-scale redistributions of population. One of the greatest spatial growth disparities is between those regions having peoples mainly of European origin (Europe, Anglo-America, U.S.S.R., and Oceania), and those with populations very largely of non-European derivation (Asia, Africa, and most of Latin America). This dichotomy differentiates more developed regions or countries from less developed ones. Even prior to 1850, the European peoples showed a slightly greater rate of increase of population than the non-Europeans. This was not so much true of

TABLE 2.5   Growth of Population in More Developed and Less Developed Areas of the World, 1850–2000

| | "Medium" Estimates | | | | Projections to 2000 | |
	1850	1900	1950	1965	"Low"	"High"
Population (millions)						
More developed areas	343	562	834	999	1,245	1,516
Less developed areas	919	1,088	1,682	2,281	4,204	5,478
Annual rate of increase since preceding date (percent)						
More developed areas	—	1.0	0.8	1.2	0.6	1.2
Less developed areas	—	0.3	0.9	2.1	1.8	2.5
Share of world total increase since preceding date (percent)						
More developed areas	—	56	31	22	11	14
Less developed areas	—	44	69	78	89	86

SOURCE: Durand, "Expansion of World Population," p. 143.

TABLE 2.6 Percentages of Population Increase in Successive Decades, 1960–2000, According to Variants of the United Nations Projections

Decade	World Total			Less Developed Areas			More Developed Areas		
	Medium	Low	High	Medium	Low	High	Medium	Low	High
1960–1970	19.8	18.2	22.0	24.1	22.4	26.5	10.8	9.6	12.9
1970–1980	20.6	17.0	24.4	25.0	21.0	29.3	10.3	7.8	12.9
1980–1990	19.8	15.3	25.0	23.4	18.6	29.7	10.4	7.0	12.6
1990–2000	18.2	13.9	22.9	21.2	17.1	26.4	9.3	4.8	12.3

SOURCE: Durand, "Expansion of World Population," p. 144.

Europe itself as it was of European stock overseas. But after about 1850, as the impact of the Scientific-Industrial Revolution began to be strongly felt, mainly of course by European peoples, the disparity between the population growth rates of the more developed and less developed realms widened, with the former growing more rapidly (Fig. 2.3). The disparity was partly a consequence of an increased rate of growth among populations of European origin and partly due to a decrease in the rate of growth of other peoples. The upward-trending growth rates of European peoples was mainly due to declining mortality, whereas the slowing growth rates of populations of non-European stock were chiefly attributable to rising mortality rates. Densely populated Asia (China and India) was largely responsible for the latter situation, for the other less developed regions of Africa and Latin America had growth rates equal to or higher than those of Europe (see Table 2.3). Thus in 1750 (Table 2.7) the more developed countries (excluding Latin America) are believed to have supported only about 21.6 percent of the earth's population (medium estimates), but this rose to 22.2 percent by 1800, 24.7 percent by 1850, and 31.4 percent by 1900. The proportion had declined by 1950. There was a similar rise in the more developed realm's share of world increase in population over the same period—24.6 percent from 1750 to 1800, 33.5 percent 1800–1850, and 53.1 percent 1850–1900 (see Tables 2.5 and 2.7).

The striking increase of population within the European culture area, together with the mounting technical skills which these peoples came to possess for exploiting natural resources and for imposing their will upon non-European peoples, made it possible for the less numerous white, or European, populations to dominate the earth. They became the masters, a fact that did not ingratiate them with the nonwhite peoples and that has continued to plague the relations between whites and non-whites down to the present.

These same features of rapid growth at home and increased mastery of natural resources led to a gargantuan outflow of peoples from Europe to the far corners of the earth. Much the largest portion of this out-migration represented a settling by Europeans of newly discovered and sparsely populated lands in middle latitudes—in North and South America, Australia, New Zealand, Asiatic U.S.S.R., and parts of the northern and southern extremities of Africa. It is estimated that the total number of Europeans migrating overseas may have exceeded 60 million, with the United States absorbing about 60 percent. Out of this large-scale migration came not only an important redistribution of the earth's people, involving a wider dissemination of the European stock, but also the establishment of a fourth world center of population concentration,

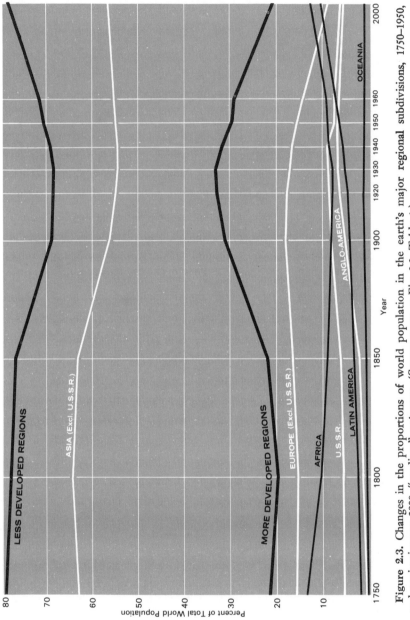

Figure 2.3. Changes in the proportions of world population in the earth's major regional subdivisions, 1750–1950, and projections to 2000, "medium" estimates. (Source same as Fig. 2.2, Table 1.)

TABLE 2.7 Growth of Population in Principal Areas of European Settlement: "Medium" Estimates, 1750–1950, and Projections to 2000

Date	Population (millions)	Share of World Total (percent)	Increase since Preceding Date	
			Annual Rate (percent)	Share of World Increase (percent)
A. Including Middle and South America				
1750	187	23.6	—	—
1800	241	24.6	0.5	28.9
1850	350	27.7	0.7	38.4
1900	592	35.9	1.1	62.4
1950	913	36.3	0.9	37.1
2000	1,904	31.1	1.5	27.4
B. Excluding Middle and South America (More Developed Countries)				
1750	171	21.6	—	—
1800	217	22.2	0.5	24.6
1850	312	24.7	0.7	33.5
1900	518	31.4	1.0	53.1
1950	751	29.9	0.7	26.9
2000	1,266	20.7	1.1	14.2

SOURCE: Durand, "Expansion of World Population," p. 141.

and a second of the white race—in east and central Anglo-America. Applying their advanced techniques to new and fertile soils, the settlers from Europe were able to produce such an abundance of food and agricultural raw materials that huge export surpluses became available for the mother countries.

In those parts of the earth where population was already dense (such as eastern and southern Asia), or where the tropical climate discouraged white agricultural settlement (as in much of Latin America and Africa, and in southern Asia), the immigrant Europeans were able to achieve political and economic domination even though their numbers remained small. Using their own skills and capital, but depending on the native labor, they developed commercial plantation agriculture, exploited mineral resources, built railroads and ports, and established trade. The products as well as the dividends from these profitable ventures went largely to Europe. The native peoples gained only a modest economic advantage from being associated with the world economy, although certain elements of European culture such as medical science, public sanitation, improved transportation, and scientific agriculture had the effect in some regions of reducing mortality rates and thereby increasing the rates of population growth.

The Demographic Transition. Incidental reference has been made earlier to the demographic transition (sometimes called the vital revolution or the demographic cycle), but it warrants somewhat greater elaboration since it is closely identified with the modern period of population history and population geography. It is, moreover, one of the most significant and best documented historical events of the last two centuries. The demographic transition appears to be one of those significant concepts which allows the organization of numerous kinds of population data into orderly and coherent patterns. And because it emphasizes the processes of temporal population change, the two concepts of time and space are both involved.

As one of the earth's animal species, man is a part of nature. Like all life, he is born, lives, and dies, and to live it is required that he satisfy certain basic needs; also he must breed and reproduce his kind if his species is to endure. But the human animal, unlike all other species, has developed culture, defined as all those qualities acquired as a member of society. Of fundamental importance is the fact that while biologically man is one, culturally he is many. It is his dual nature, combining as it does cultural diversity and biological unity, that accounts for some of the outstanding features of population history in the modern period, including those differentials between fertility and mortality, which in turn determine rate of natural increase.

By means of generalizing principles involving sequential changes in fertility and mortality, a useful typology or model of stages in population growth has been evolved. This is called the demographic transition model (Fig. 2.4). All nations which during the modern era have passed from a traditional, agriculturally oriented economy to one that is strongly industrial and urban have at the same time evolved from a condition of high fertility and mortality to one where both of these vital rates are relatively low. In the process of making this change, nearly all have experienced an intermediate stage, of variable length, where mortality is well below fertility, resulting in remarkable increases in population numbers and striking changes in the relative proportions of the young, middle-aged, and old (Fig. 2.4). Other associated changes, partly cause and partly effect, occurred in the proportions of rural and urban dwellers, in the investment patterns, in the proportions of con-

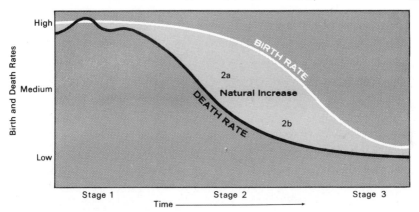

Figure 2.4. The demographic transition model.

sumers to producers, and in the relation of population to natural re-sources. Relevant to the preceding generalizations, Stolnitz makes the following observations.[8] The period of time required for consummation of the transition, while varying widely between countries, is a relatively long-time affair, involving two or more quarters of a century, or several generations. The rapidity of change to lower modern vital rates represents a highly important break with the past. The trends toward lower vital rates appear to be irreversible except temporarily, or as a result of catastrophies. The present low vital rates characteristic of Western countries could have been attained by various routes through time. But of unusual significance is the fact that mortality decline usually has either preceded or was more rapid than that of natality, with a large increase in numbers resulting. The demographic transition has been modified in some regions by large-scale migration; out-migration in the case of Europe, and in-migration in the instances of Anglo-America, nontropical Latin America, and Oceania. And, finally, it must be emphasized that a large majority of the earth's population, the two-thirds to three-fourths in the less developed realm, has not yet completed the demographic transition; there is still no evidence of a fertility decline in a vast majority of the world's less developed people (Fig. 2.5). Hence their rate of growth is unparalleled and no genuine relief is in sight.

The heartland of the transition process is northwestern and central Europe and the emigrant populations of these regions overseas in Anglo-

[8] George J. Stolnitz, The Demographic Transition: From High to Low Birth Rates and Death Rates. In Ronald Freedman (ed.), *Population: The Vital Revolution*, Aldine, Chicago, 1965. Chap. 2, pp. 30–46.

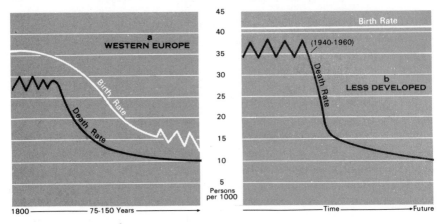

Figure 2.5. Schematic presentation of birth and death rates; A, for Western Europe after 1800; B, for the less developed countries in the mid-twentieth century. The steep decline in the death rate from about 35 per 1000 began at varying times between 1940 and 1960 for different less developed countries. (From "The Population Council 1952–1964," a report, July 1965; Elements of Geography by Trewartha, Robinson and Hammond. McGraw-Hill.)

America, Australia, and New Zealand. Only since World War II have eastern and southern Europe, Japan, and temperate South America completed or nearly completed the transition. In the greatly different social, economic, and political environment of eastern and southern Europe not only was the timing of the transition different and briefer, but in some ways it is less complete. Over a period of only somewhat more than a decade, from the early 1920s to the late 1930s, birth rates in southern and eastern Europe dropped by amounts it took western Europe 30 to 60 years to achieve. There is some indirect evidence that mortality in the West may have shown a weak and fluctuating downward trend during the century or two preceding the Industrial Revolution. The course of fertility is even more uncertain, but at any rate the earliest figures available on national birth rates in Western countries are well below those of today's traditional societies. Sweden by about 1750, and France by about 1800, had reached a *relatively* low fertility level of 30–35 per 1000. By about 1850 most of the West had experienced a sort of preliminary demographic transition, whose timing and causes remain obscure for individual countries.

After a rather long lull in demographic change in the middle decades of the nineteenth century, the last quarter witnessed remarkable activity in the form of an unusually rapid decline in both fertility and mortality in most Western countries, with associated large increases in population.

After about 1860–1875 mortality rates were continuously downward, while declining fertility trends gathered momentum over several decades. In some parts of the West fertility rose again, but only temporarily, after World War II.

Three or four main population stages in the demographic transition are usually recognized, but they are named differently by various authors. Here they are designated (1) preindustrial, (2) early Western, and (3) late Western (Fig. 2.4). The first of these, the preindustrial stage, is characteristic of traditional cultures that have not been modified significantly by modern Western science and technology. Included are all cultures antedating the Industrial Revolution, as well as any contemporary ones not considerably influenced by the West. Such a type prevailed among all cultures throughout the millenniums of human history, excepting the last two or three centuries. Its extreme form resembled animal living. Birth rates were typically high, life was precarious, many died in infancy, length of life was under 35 years, and death rates were high and fluctuating. There was approximate balance between fertility and mortality, so that natural increase was static or slow. Nevertheless, the growth potential was high. Until the last decade or two black Africa, the area south of the Sahara, remained the last major stronghold of the demographic transition's stage 1. But the very recent and widespread penetration of Western medicine and sanitation has resulted in a falling death rate in so many parts that the area has become transitional in character, with probably more of its population falling within stage 2 than stage 1. To be sure, reliable mortality statistics

TABLE 2.8 Three Conceptual Types of Society and Their Characteristics

Stage	Fertility	Mortality	Population Growth	Economy
1. Preindustrial	High	High and fluctuating	Static to low	Primitive or agricultural
2. Early Western	High	Falling	High	Mixed
3. Modern Western	Controlled— usually low to moderate	Low	Low to moderate	Urban-industrial and mixed

SOURCE: Modified from Petersen, *Population*, p. 12.

are lacking for many African states, but the best estimates suggest that a majority of the Negro countries probably now have crude death rates under 30 per 1000.

The early Western stage, number 2, is characterized by imbalance between births and deaths. The decline in deaths precedes and is more rapid than the falling off in births, resulting in a large natural increase. This stage follows from a gradual reduction of hunger and disease, and often a general improvement in health and standards of living. Mortality falls rapidly, while for some time fertility continues to be high, and the two rates diverge. Later in this intermediate stage, planned fertility control reduces birth rates, while death decline slackens relatively. There is a converging of the two rates, causing natural increase to slow down somewhat. Thus two subtypes of stage 2, may be recognized (see Fig. 2.4).

In the third, or modern Western stage, both fertility and mortality are controlled. In large measure, babies are born only to parents who want them. Death rates are low and birth rates normally are low to moderate. This third stage resembles the first in that a fair balance between births and deaths usually has been achieved, and the natural increase is not excessive as it is likely to be in stage 2. But while stages 1 and 3 both normally represent a low-to-moderate natural increase, they differ in that growth potential is high in stage 1, low in stage 3.

The first stage in the demographic transition has been likened to a taut coiled spring under restraint; stage 2 to the rapid expansion of the spring following removal of the restraining force; and stage 3 to the slack spring after its force has been spent.

Stage 1, exemplified by people who have had only slight contact with Western culture, represents a rapidly shrinking part of the earth's modern population. As Western medicine has spread quickly through the less developed regions, no very large numbers of people in Latin America and Asia remain in this stage. But since Africa was the last population cluster to emerge from it, which it only recently did, it is there, in all probability, that the largest numbers, or at least the largest percentages, still persist. Stage 2 is at present representative of two-thirds to three-quarters of the earth's people (Type 1, Fig. 2.6). They dwell mainly in the three underdeveloped continents and are overwhelmingly nonwhites. Stage 3 is typical of peoples of European culture and, in addition, Japan, where science and technology are well advanced. They represent about one-quarter to one-third of humanity (Type 2, Fig. 2.6).

Although the model of the demographic transition, with its 3 stages as given above, is a useful generalization having widespread applicability, it is not universally relevant. It does not even represent with great ac-

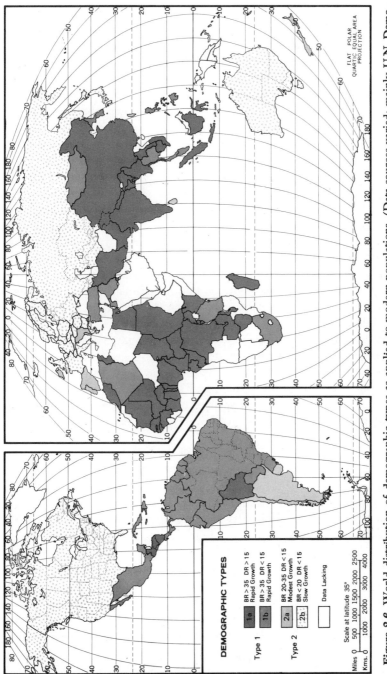

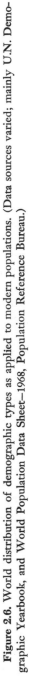

Figure 2.6. World distribution of demographic types as applied to modern populations. (Data sources varied; mainly U.N. Demographic Yearbook, and World Population Data Sheet–1968, Population Reference Bureau.)

DEMOGRAPHIC TYPES

Type 1
- 1a — BR > 35 DR > 15 Rapid Growth
- 1b — BR > 35 DR < 15 Rapid Growth

Type 2
- 2a — BR 20-35 DR < 15 Modest Growth
- 2b — BR < 20 DR < 15 Slow Growth

Data Lacking

Scale at latitude 35°
Miles 0 500 1000 1500 2000 2500
Kms. 0 1000 2000 3000 4000

FLAT POLAR QUARTIC EQUAL AREA PROJECTION

49

curacy the population history of the West and there is no assurance that it will strongly resemble in most respects those of the less developed regions. Certainly it is too gross a simplification to reflect accurately the population history of individual Western countries. For example, much of western Europe did not start from the high-fertility plateau assumed in the model. Even late medieval and early modern Europe had built-in controls that operated to hold down the average birth rate. And, as noted earlier, in most Western countries there was probably an initial increase in family size before the long-continued downward trend in fertility set in. In this respect, France and the United States are exceptions, for in France a trend toward smaller families was perceptible even in the second half of the eighteenth century, and in the United States early in the nineteenth. For England, the transition model functions much better for the period after about 1850, when scientific medicine and public sanitation combined rapidly to lower mortality. In the beginning it was even assumed the demographic transition model could be used for predictive purposes. One prediction was that fertility decline would continue until a stationary stage was reached, so the marked upturn in birth rates after 1945 in some Western countries, including the United States, was unexpected.

Roy Chung has attempted to treat the demographic transition model in a geographical way.[9] On a series of 11 world maps he has shown the distribution, by national units, of the three stages of the transition model, beginning with 1905–1909 pentad, and by 5-year intervals from then to 1960. These maps show which parts or countries of the earth were in any one of the three transition stages in any one of the 11 specified periods within the twentieth century.

To what extent the less developed nations will conform to the model of the demographic transition is only conjecture. It may be significant in this respect that, with some modifications, the model has been approximately followed by Japan, the single important nonwhite nation to have accomplished the demographic transition. In the West, mortality decline was experienced gradually, the result of a series of death-delaying discoveries. Such a step-by-step procedure is not being followed in the less developed countries where the latest discoveries of Western medicine and pharmacy are applied without an accompanying change in social structure. As a result mortality has plummeted even in simple agrarian societies and among primitive peoples. Death controls suddenly have been made available to even the least advanced (see

[9] Roy Chung, Space-Time Diffusion of the Transition Model: The Twentieth Century Patterns. Paper read at meeting of the Population Association of America, New York City, April 30, 1966.

Fig. 2.5). The effects may be catastrophic. If fertility remains high and constant in the developing nations, or declines no faster than it did in the West, unmanageable increases in population numbers will result. Moreover, some regions, especially Asia, start out with numbers and densities of people far in excess of those in the West at the beginning of their stage of rapid growth, so that the multiplication of human life and resulting population pressure will be far greater. What is more, the West's period of rapid multiplication coincided with a transforming economy that was able to support many more people and at a higher standard of living. This is not the case in Asia, Africa, and Latin America where traditional living is contemporaneous with a plummeting death rate. Hence disaster in the form of famine and epidemics is a real threat and there is no certainty that catastrophic losses in human life can be avoided. On the hopeful side is the fact that much more is known now about birth control than was true a century ago, and efficient means of mass communication are available for disseminating the information, so just possibly fertility decline may be initiated at an earlier economic stage than it was in the West.

Furthermore, not all less developed nations can be expected to follow similar patterns of population change. For while they all lack the long preparation for modernization that the West built on, they differ significantly among themselves. Most Latin American countries begin modernization with only modest population numbers and densities, and with a culture that involves a Western language and stronger Western influences than Africa and Asia. By contrast, Asia has far greater numbers and overall densities, a much longer and more distinguished history, a far more intensive and efficient agriculture, but a language and culture that are Oriental. Black Africa is not as burdened with numbers as is Asia, but its political, economic, and social organization is at a lower level than either Asia's or Latin America's.

A final reason why predictions based upon a model of the demographic transition may fail for the less developed countries is that government policy decisions now influence demographic trends far more than was true in the more laissez-faire West of the nineteenth century. No doubt social planning will continue and probably intensify. Its consequence, both in goals and in methods, cannot be foreseen.

Different growth rates have occurred at particular periods over the past three centuries because of timing differences in the demographic transition between regions of advanced European settlement and those of nonwhite, less developed peoples. Since, with the exception of Japan, people of European origin are the only ones to have completed the demographic transition, it is they who have already passed the middle

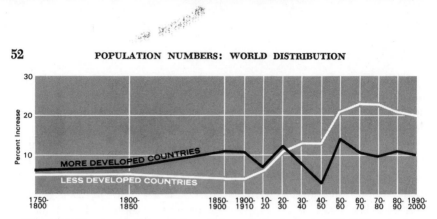

Figure 2.7. Comparative rates of decennial population increase 1750–1950, and projections to 2000, "medium estimates," for the less developed and the more developed parts of the world. (*Sources: World Population Estimates, 1750–2000,* United Nations Doc. WPC/WP/289; *Provisional Report on World Population Prospects as Assessed in 1963,* United Nations, 1964.)

stage of rapid growth and have arrived at the last stage where deaths are low, births moderate or low, and rate of population increase moderate or low (Fig. 2.7). They are no longer growing rapidly in numbers as they did during the nineteenth century, and at present their rate of increase is below the world average.

By contrast, the non-European or colored peoples, who were affected by the Scientific-Industrial Revolution later, are today less advanced in the demographic transition. They are mainly in stage 2, where continuing high birth rates and plummeting, or in some areas already low, death rates keep natural increase high. So the comparative growth rates between more developed and less developed peoples, which favored the former for most of the modern period, have been reversed during the most recent past decades. It is the colored peoples whose growth rates are now in the ascendancy (Figs. 2.7; 2.3).

Population Change and Future Growth. Table 2.9 gives the gross regional patterns of population change over two centuries of the modern period. It must be cautioned that all figures for the earlier dates are only estimates, and those for Africa, Asia, and Latin America even for later dates are based upon slim evidence.

For a time span of somewhat under 200 years following 1750 the regions of European settlement (excluding Latin America), or what is here called the more developed realm, increased their proportion (21.6 percent in 1750 to 32.7 in 1930) of the earth's total population, while the regions of non-European settlement lost proportionally (78.4 percent to 67.3). Since then, as noted previously, the two trends have reversed direction (Fig. 2.7). Between 1920 and 1960 the aggregate population of the less developed regions is estimated to have increased by about

TABLE 2.9 Percentage of World Population by Major Regions

	1750	1800	1850	1900	1920	1930	1940	1950	1960	2000
More Developed Areas	21.6	22.1	24.7	31.4	32.6	32.7	31.8	29.8	28.6	20.7
Europe	15.8	15.5	16.5	17.9	17.6	17.1	16.5	15.6	14.2	8.6
Soviet Union	5.3	5.7	6.0	8.1	8.3	8.6	8.5	7.1	7.2	5.8
Anglo-America	.25	.7	2.1	5.0	6.2	6.5	6.3	6.6	6.7	5.8
Oceania	.25	.2	.16	0.4	0.5	0.5	0.5	0.5	0.5	0.5
Less Developed Regions	78.4	77.8	75.3	68.6	67.4	67.3	68.2	70.2	71.4	79.3
Asia (exc. U.S.S.R.)	63.0	64.4	63.5	56.1	54.9	54.2	54.2	54.9	55.2	56.4
Africa	13.4	10.9	8.8	8.1	7.7	7.9	8.3	8.8	9.1	12.5
Latin America	2.0	2.5	3.0	4.5	4.8	5.2	5.7	6.5	7.1	10.4

SOURCE: Compiled from Durand, "Expansion of Population," Table 1, p. 137 and U.N., *World Population Prospects*, 1964, Table 5.2, p. 40.

70 percent, the more developed regions by only about 40 percent. During the same four decades the less developed nations increased their share of world population from about 67 to 71 percent; that of the developed regions declined from 33 to 29. According to the United Nation's "medium" estimates, the post-1930 trends are expected to continue until at least 2000, at which time the ratio of the earth's total population in the developed to underdeveloped realms will be approximately 21:79. Within the more developed realm Europe's (excluding the U.S.S.R.) proportion grew only modestly until the early 1900s, after which it declined, so that in 1950 it was very similar to what it was two centuries earlier (see Fig. 2.3). The decline in its proportion of world population is expected to continue to at least 2000, at which time it will reach a low of 8–9 percent. The U.S.S.R. increased its proportion more rapidly than did the rest of Europe, so that whereas the ratio of Europe to U.S.S.R. was about 3:1 in 1750, it was just about 2:1 between 1930 and 1960. Soviet Russia's proportion has declined since about 1930, and will probably continue to decline, but not as rapidly as that of the rest of Europe. Anglo-America's proportion of the earth's population rose spectacularly during the century and a half following 1750, then slowed in the 1900s, and has reached something of a plateau between 1920 and 1960. A modest decline is anticipated by 2000 (Table 2.10).

Among the non-European regions, Asia, the population giant, lost ground in its proportion of the earth's population from the mid-eighteenth century to about 1940; there has since been a slow rise, which is expected to continue to 2000 (see Fig. 2.3). If the estimates for Africa may be considered a sufficiently accurate base for comparisons, that continent declined in its proportion of the earth's population for a century or more after 1750. A low appears to have been reached in about 1920, after which the trend has been upward, more rapidly than in Asia but less so than in Latin America. Of the three great less developed continents, Latin America is exceptional, for since 1750 its proportion of humanity has constantly increased, and with ever-increasing rapidity. It was only 2 percent in 1750, 3 percent in 1800, 4.3 percent in 1900, and 6.5 percent in 1950. By 2000 its proportion is expected to reach 10.4 percent (Table 2.9).

If the anticipated trends in birth and death rates continue, the earth's population will become decreasingly white and increasingly colored for some time to come. The implications of this politically charged fact are enormous, for it is the more developed, or predominantly white nations with only one-fourth to one-third of the population that produce and consume more than two-thirds of the world's goods, while a large proportion of the much more populous nonwhites live in poverty, ignorance,

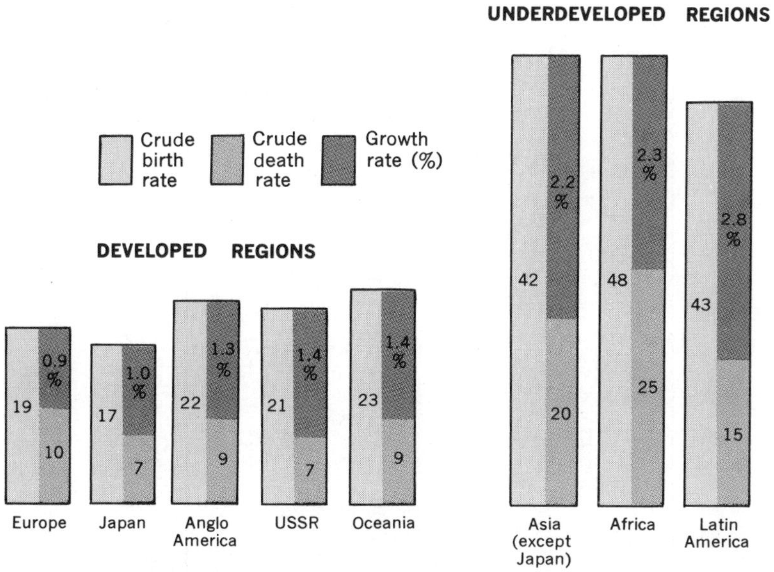

Figure 2.8. Estimated vital rates for the earth's principal regions, separated into the less developed and more developed groups. From Elements of Geography by Trewartha, Robinson and Hammond. McGraw-Hill.

and ill health (Fig. 2.8). Moreover, these so-called have-not peoples in the backward countries have only recently become aware of the contrast between their impoverished condition and that of the wealthy white nations, and they are not willing to accept their situation as being unalterable, or even to believe that improvement must be slow. They demand not just change, but prompt change.

A serious complication which acts to stifle improvement of living standards for Asiatics, Africans, and tropical Latin Americans is their burgeoning populations, that is, their continuing high birth rates combined with falling, or in some parts even low, death rates. In Latin America, for example, while the gross national product has about doubled in the approximately two decades since 1945, general economic well-being has been slow in improving because of a more than 45 percent increase in population. During the 5 years ending with 1964, population in this region increased by 11.5 percent while food production rose only 6.5 percent, thus resulting in a reduced per capita food production of nearly 5 percent. In the much more populous Far East during the same 5-year period, population rose 10 percent but food production only 8.5 (Fig. 2.9). Thus there is a relentlessly widening disparity in wealth and population between the more developed and less developed countries,

TABLE 2.10 Decennial Changes in World Population from 1900 to 2000 Based on 1960 Levels of Economic Development (Medium Variant Estimates)

	1900	1910	1920	1930	1940	1950	1960	1970	1980	1990	2000
						(Millions)					
More developed countries [a]	518	565	606	678	730	751	854	946	1,042	1,153	1,266
Less developed countries [b]	1,132	1,190	1,256	1,392	1,565	1,766	2,136	2,628	3,227	3,915	4,699
Total	1,650	1,755	1,862	2,070	2,295	2,517	2,990	3,574	4,269	5,068	5,965

Percent Increase

	1900–1910	1910–1920	1920–1930	1930–1940	1940–1950	1950–1960	1960–1970	1970–1980	1980–1990	1990–2000
More developed countries [a]	11	7	12	8	3	14	11	10	11	10
Less developed countries [b]	4	6	11	13	13	21	23	23	21	20
Total	6	6	11	11	10	19	20	19	19	18

SOURCE: Data for 1900 derived from Durand, "Expansion of World Population," p. 137; data for 1920–2000 from U.N., *World Population Prospects,* Tables 5.1 and 5.5; data for 1910 estimated by interpolation.

[a] Europe, Oceania, U.S. and Canada, and U.S.S.R.
[b] Africa, Asia (excluding U.S.S.R.), and Latin America.

56

TABLE 2.11   Decennial Changes in the Populations of Less Developed
Regions (Medium Variant Estimates)

	1920–1930	1930–1940	1940–1950	1950–1960	1960–1970	1970–1980	1980–1990	1990–2000
				Percent				
All less developed countries	11	13	13	21	23	23	21	20
East Asia	7 [a]	7 [a]	8 [a]	16 [a]	15	14	12	10
South Asia	13	15	14	23	27	25	23	21
Africa	15 [a]	17 [a]	16 [a]	23 [a]	27	30	31	31
Latin America	20	21	25	30	33	32	31	28

SOURCE: U.N., *World Population Prospects,* Tables 5.1 and 5.6.
[a] Estimates insecure.

with all the frictions and tensions that this entails. But there can be
no solution to the economic aid and the trade problems of the less developed nations until more of them are willing to face their population
problem realistically and act to solve it. But at the same time the hungry
nations must receive hugely increased and much wiser assistance from
the affluent nations if the food gap is to be closed.

More optimism exists today than ever before concerning the prospects
for easing somewhat the impending world population crisis before the
end of the present century. To be sure, it is likely there will be a further
reduction in death rates in the less developed countries, but birth rates
are expected to decline even more rapidly, with the result that rates of
natural increase may be slowed. Thus, according to the United Nations' "medium" estimates, crude birth rates for the world will decline
from 34 in 1960–1965 to 26 in 1995–2000, from 20 to 18 for the more
developed regions, and from 40 to 28 for the less developed parts.[10] The
increased optimism in some quarters concerning a likelihood for moderat-
ing the world population crisis stems from a number of factors, including
more efficient and cheaper contraceptive devices, the degrees of ac-
ceptance of family planning by native peoples, the number of national
planning programs recently put into operation, and the improvement of
economic conditions in a number of the less developed countries. Donald
Bogue [11] has even gone so far as to predict that the world population

[10] *World Population Prospects as Assessed in 1963.* United Nations Population
Study No. 41, New York, 1966, p. 34.
[11] Donald J. Bogue, "The End of the Population Explosion," *Public Interest,*
No. 7, 1967, pp. 11–20.

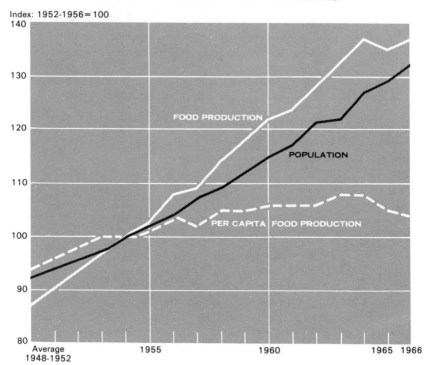

Figure 2.9. Recent rates of growth for world population, world food production, and per capita food production. Note that while food production has increased rapidly, this has been offset by population growth. As a consequence per capita food production has barely held its own, or even declined. Hunger is becoming increasingly prevalent in many of the less developed countries. (From *Population Bulletin*, December, 1968.)

crisis, so formidable a twentieth-century problem, will be largely a matter of history by the beginning of the twenty-first century. Most demographers do not share his exuberant optimism and are more restrained in their forecasts. The United Nations' projected vital rates for the less developed realm between 1960–1965 and 1995–2000, based on "medium" estimates, are as follows: crude birth rates down from 40.4 to 28.0; death rates from 19.2 to 9.2; and natural increase rates from 21.2 to 18.8.[12] This would be a remarkable accomplishment. Still, even at these declining rates there will be a gigantic population increase in the less developed realm during the 30–35 years before the end of the century. Moreover, the natural increase rate of nearly 19 per 1000 expected to be reached by 1995–2000 still allows for a doubling of population numbers

[12] U.N., *World Population Prospects,*" p. 36.

over a span of about 37 years. Clearly, a substantially reduced natality, and its associated slightly lower rate of growth, are by no means a solution of the population problem of those less developed countries, already densely populated. Yet the elements for eventual success—widespread economic and social progress, improved technology, government action —are accumulating. "It is a reasonable prediction that these will succeed and that, before the end of the century, most of the developing countries will be well along the transition to lower fertility and some relief from the problems of continuing rapid population growth." [13]

THE MAP OF WORLD POPULATION AS OF ABOUT MID-NINETEENTH CENTURY

Estimates suggest that in the two centuries following 1650 the earth's population may have increased as much as 2.7 times; that of the area of European settlement more than tripled. By far the greatest *absolute* gains occurred in the two massive Old World centers of population, with Asia, chiefly the east and south, adding an estimated 450–550 million and Europe 150–200 million in the period of 200 years. Thus Asia and Europe may have doubled to tripled the numbers of their inhabitants over the two centuries. Behm and Hanemann's density map of world population distribution, dated 1873, and, according to the authors, based upon the most recent census figures and estimates available at that time, is probably the best overall representation of how the earth's possible 12.6 hundred million people were spread over the earth's surface at mid-nineteenth century or a little later.[14] This map reveals a pattern whose gross lineaments show many features that prevailed nearly two millenniums earlier, as well as those of a present-day map of population distribution. Conspicuous are the two vast Asiatic centers of high density, one in eastern Asia and the other in the Indian subcontinent, concentrations which have endured for nearly 2000 years. Equally prominent is the high-density center in Europe. Beginning to emerge, but still not striking, is a fourth center, in eastern and central Anglo-America, with the highest densities concentrated along the Atlantic seaboard from

[13] Dudley Kirk, *Natality in the Developing Countries.* Manuscript of paper prepared for Fertility and Family Planning: A World View, University of Michigan Sesquicentennial Celebration, Ann Arbor, Nov. 15–17, 1967, p. 23.

[14] E. Behm and H. Wagner, *Die Bevölkerung der Erde,* Erganzungsheft No. 35, Erganzungsband No. 8 zu *Petermann's Geographischen Mitteilungen,* Justus Perthes, Gotha, 1874; mit Zwei Karten: Tafel 1, E. Behm and F. Hanemann, Die Verteilung der Menschen über die Erde, Massstab, 1:80,000,000; Tafel 2, Dichtickeit der Bevölkerung in Europa, Massstab, 1:11,000,000.

southern New England to Washington, D.C. Most likely the concentration of population shown for western tropical Africa is exaggerated on the Behm and Hanemann map, a consequence of using inflated population figures for the African continent. This feature will be commented upon later.

Old-World Population. Considering the very low reliability of any population estimates for Asia for 1650, and the wide range in the 1850 estimates for that continent, it is almost futile to attempt to construct the growth rates for Asia over the first two centuries of the modern period. Still, any and all estimates indicate that Asia in 1650, and also in 1850, supported half to two-thirds of the earth's people, and it is likely to have increased its share of humanity during that span of two centuries. By far the largest part of the continent's people were located along its eastern and southern margins where there were four regions of remarkably high density; China, India, Japan, and Java—a situation strikingly similar to the modern one.

It is generally accepted that in China, following the establishment of the Manchu Dynasty in the middle of the seventeenth century, there was a long period of general prosperity and probably of population increase. Ching Chang-heng estimated the mid-seventeenth century population base of the Chinese Empire as between 76 and 95 million.[15] Recorded official estimates suggest an empire population of about 430 million in 1850.[16] It is, of course, almost impossible to make judgments concerning the magnitude and rate of population growth in modern China, but growth appears at least to have been fairly rapid. Knowledge of how this increased population was distributed must be based upon the still more shaky evidence provided by provincial estimates. But employing Durand's amended provincial estimates,[17] which indicate for 1851 a population of 428.7 million for China proper (including Taiwan) and 3.2 million for the outlying areas, we find 124 million, or 29 percent, were located in the six provinces of North China as of the mid-nineteenth century. This approximates the degree of concentration in the same region according to the census of 1953, a century later. In addition to the extensive area of high density in North China, roughly coincident with the delta of the Hwang River, Shantung, and the Loess Highlands, the Behm and Hanemann map shows other large concentrations of population, with accompanying high densities, in the Yangtze Basin, the

15 John D. Durand, "The Population Statistics of China, A.D.–1953." *Population Studies*, Vol. 13, 1960, p. 237.
16 Durand, "Population Statistics," p. 240.
17 Durand, "Population Statistics," p. 251.

Szechwan Basin, and along the southeast coast. Thus by 1850 China had become by far the most populous country in Asia, indeed, in the whole world, greatly exceeding the Indian center in South Asia, and probably containing about one-third of the earth's people.

Accepting Moreland's estimate of an Indian population of at least 100 million in the early seventeenth century, and after adjusting the census returns of 1871, Davis postulates an expansion of the subcontinent's population from 100 to 255 million over the two-and-one-half centuries.[18] Thus the Indian population center by around 1850, although much smaller than that of China, still must have contained almost one-fifth of the earth's people. Behm and Hanemann show the chief concentration of high densities in the humid parts of the Indus-Ganges lowland, on the coastal lowlands flanking the eastern margins of peninsular India, and in the southern part of the Deccan. In India as well as China, therefore, the distribution of people about a century ago bears strong resemblance to what it is today.

Although dwarfed in magnitude by the Chinese and Indian populations of the mid-nineteenth century, Japan's 20–30 million inhabitants nevertheless represented a small center of relatively high density. By 1726 Nippon's population had reached 26–27 million, but it changed little in the next century and a quarter.[19] This static population represented an approach to near saturation, or the limits imposed by subsistence agriculture at the then existing technical levels.[20]

In Southeast Asia, where the overall density was much lower than that in China, India, and Japan, as it continues to be even now, the Java center, with an estimated population of 6,000,000 in about 1830, was the exception. By official estimate the 1860–1870 population had reached nearly 17 million, representing a density of about 125 per square kilometer,[21] or higher than that of Japan.

Any estimates of Africa's population several centuries back can be little more than guesses. Both Willcox and Carr-Saunders offer the figure of 100 million for 1650, while Durand suggests only 111 million as of two centuries later. If one accepts these estimates, then the African section of Behm and Hanemann's map of world population must show exaggerated densities, since they use a figure for total population (203

---

[18] Kingsley Davis, *The Population of India and Pakistan*, Princeton University Press, Princeton, N.J., 1952, p. 16.

[19] Irene B. Taeuber, *The Population of Japan*, Princeton University Press, Princeton, N.J., 1958, p. 20.

[20] Taeuber, *Population of Japan*, pp. 21–22.

[21] Behm and Wagner, *Bevölkerung*, pp. 44–45.

TABLE 2.12 Population of Europe by Major Subdivisions

Regions	Area Million Km²	Percent of Continent	Population (Millions) 1720	1820	1870	1900	1930	Percent Population of Europe 1720	1820	1870	1900	1930
Western Europe (Inc. Switzerland)	0.93	9.6	32	59	81	98	107	32	28	27	25	22
Central Europe	1.52	15.7	25	56	81	114	148	25	27	27	29	30
Scandinavian and Baltic Lands	1.32	13.6	3	8	12	16	22	3	4	4	4	4
Mediterranean Peninsulas	1.44	14.8	24	50	63	79	100	24	24	21	20	20
U.S.S.R. (European)	4.50	46.3	16	37	63	86	120	16	17	21	22	24
Europe Total			110	209	300	392	497	100	100	100	100	100

SOURCE: Haliczer, "Population of Europe," pp. 261–273.

million) nearly double that of Durand's for 1850. On the Behm and Hanemann map three general areas of population concentration in Africa are indicated; one in the extreme north along the Mediterranean Sea margins; another in the extreme south and southeast, and the third, much larger and more important, in humid, tropical Africa south of the Sahara. It is the last area, in all probability, with its estimated 157 million people, which has been most exaggerated in numbers and therefore in overall density.

Australia, on the eve of a rapid natural and immigrant population increase during the third quarter of the nineteenth century, supported fewer than 1.5 million people in mid-century, and these were concentrated in a small number of isolated clusters around port cities along the southeastern rimland.

As noted earlier, Europe's population multiplied more rapidly in the first two centuries of the modern era than did that of the earth as a whole, and grew from an estimated 100 million in 1650 (Willcox's figure) to 284 million in 1850 (Durand's figure). But growth within Europe was far from being uniform, as indicated in Table 2.12. Thus while all five of the principal continental subdivisions gained in absolute numbers, the two older centers in western and Mediterranean Europe were growing less rapidly than central and eastern Europe, so that their relative proportions of the continent's people waned while those to the east and north increased. The center of gravity of population in Europe was moving eastward and slightly northward (Fig. 2.10).[22]

Perhaps the outstanding feature, however, was the continuing reenforcement that occurred within two belts of higher density, already in evidence at the beginning of the nineteenth century, which cut across four of the five major regional subdivisions of the continent (Fig. 2.11). The two population axes, one trending north-south and the other more east-west, intersected in Flanders. Each contained areas where population density exceeded 100 per square kilometer (260 per square mile).[23] The one having a N-S alignment reached from northern Ireland on the west, through England and the Rhineland, to northern Italy, interrupted by the Alps. The other, with an E-W direction, extended from Britanny, through northern France, southern Germany, Bohemia, southern Poland, and, in weaker form, eastward into the U.S.S.R. Sparseness of cities and towns was notable in the eastern parts of the E-W belt, but they were more numerous in the west and also in Italy. Of the areas with marked

[22] Joseph Haliczer, "The Population of Europe, 1720, 1820, 1930," *Geography*, Vol. XIX, 1934, pp. 261–273 (esp. p. 272).
[23] Alan G. Ogilvie, *Europe and Its Borderlands*. Thomas Nelson and Sons, Edinburgh, 1957, pp. 243–244.

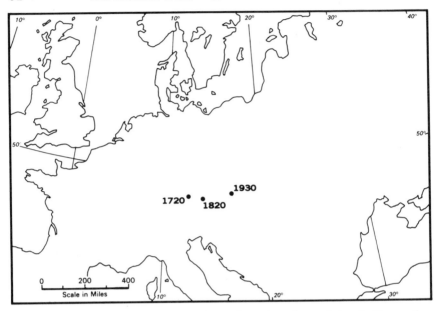

Figure 2.10. The location of the center of gravity of population in Europe has shifted eastward over the two centuries since 1720. (From Joseph Haliczer, "The Population of Europe, 1720, 1820, 1930," *Geography*, Vol. 19, 1934.)

concentrations of towns, two were old, those in Flanders and Italy, while one was new, that of England.[24] In France and Flanders this concentration had already been established toward the end of the Middle Ages. But as late as 1720 the chernozem zone in eastern Europe was almost empty.[25] This east-west belt was a foothill zone all the way from the valleys of the Sambre and Meuse in the west to the base of the Carpathians in the east. Even before the modern exploitation of coal, lignite, and potash had converted this zone into an important industrial belt with numerous cities, it had supported a relatively dense rural population, for it represented a belt of fertile loam soil, much of it of loessial origin (Fig. 2.12). The adjoining hills saw the rise of metals mining in Europe and also small industries based upon the use of local water power.[26] The north-south population belt followed the Rhine Valley northward from the Swiss plateau, but with extensions into the basin of the Neckar, along the valley of the Main, and north through Hesse to the Fulda and Weser valleys. This was a region of small farms, inten-

[24] Ogilvie, *Europe*, p. 244.
[25] Haliczer, "Population of Europe," p. 263.
[26] Haliczer, "Population of Europe," p. 235.

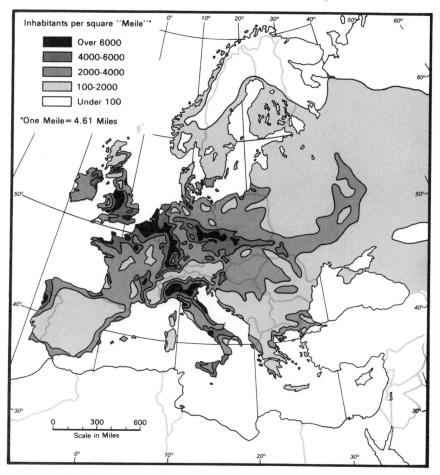

Figure 2.11. Population density in Europe in the third quarter of the nineteenth century. (Modified from map by E. Behm and H. Wagner, in *Petermann's Geographischen Metteilungen*, Enganzungsheft No. 35, 1874, Tafel 2.)

sively cultivated, of numerous and varied industries, and a close network of communications.[27]

Thus the seventeenth to mid-nineteenth centuries saw not so much a redistribution of people in Europe, but rather a further piling up of the 200 million population growth along the E-W and N-S axes of population developed earlier. To be sure, the E-W axis had been extended deeper into Russia as the eastern reaches of the fertile chernozem belt increasingly came under cultivation. The peopling of these areas of fertile grassland

[27] Ogilvie, *Europe,* p. 235.

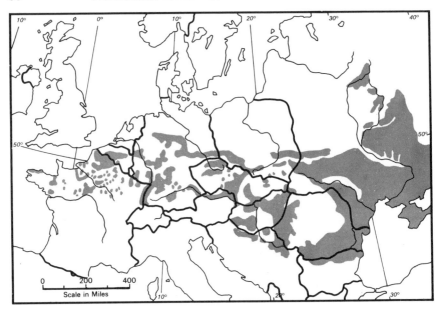

Figure 2.12. Distribution of loess in Europe. (After a map by R. Gradmann.)

soils farther east, almost empty as late as 1720, and containing only discontinuous centers of important settlement by 1820, was a major event of the population geography of the nineteenth century.[28]   Only in Britain, where the revolution in industry and transport began earliest, had manufacturing and population undergone a drastic regional localization by 1870. On the continent the development of large urban clusters and the regional concentration of industries and population were not nearly so advanced. Thus, by 1871–1872 almost 62 percent of the people of England and Wales lived in towns and cities of more than 2,000 people; the comparable figures for Germany and France were 36 and 31 percent.[29] In Britain there were numerous new cities whose origin had been stimulated by manufacturing. On the continent most urban centers were old, and had originated as provincial and state capitals, seaports, and inland trade centers in an earlier period. Many of the industrial cities on the mainland are post-1870 phenomena.[30]

New-World Population.   As a consequence of both immigration and natural increase, population in the New World grew from an estimated

[28] Haliczer, "Population of Europe," p. 268.
[29] W. Gordon East, *An Historical Geography of Europe*, Methuen, London, 1938, p. 414.
[30] East, *Historical Geography*, p. 415.

13 million (Carr-Saunders' figure) in the mid-seventeenth century to about 64 million (Durand's figure) two centuries later. The indigenous population did not share importantly in this growth; indeed the native peoples may actually have declined in numbers, or, as was the case in Latin America, blended in large numbers with the European and African immigrants to produce an important element of mixed blood.

Of the estimated 38 million persons living in Latin America in 1850, perhaps 40 percent were in Middle America and 60 percent in South America. In the former the principal concentration was in the southern part of the Mexican central plateau, with much smaller centers of population in Honduras, El Salvador, and some of the Caribbean islands.

As of the mid-nineteenth century, South America's estimated 22–23 million inhabitants were strongly concentrated in a Brazilian coastal zone extending southward from the mouth of the Amazon. Three centers were conspicuous; one in the northeast around Pernambuco-Baía; a second around Rio de Janeiro-Sao Paulo, and a third in Minas Gerais. Another peripheral zone of higher density occupied the coasts and the Andean basins and uplands from Venezuela and Colombia on the north, southward through Ecuador and Peru, to Bolivia, along the Pacific margins. Somewhat isolated centers of above-average density were coincident with the vale of central Chile, the oases of dry northern Argentina, parts of the eastern Pampas near Buenos Aires, and central Paraguay around Asunción. The most conspicuous feature of population distribution in South America as of about the mid-nineteenth century, one clearly apparent on the Behm and Hanemann map, was the strong concentration of settlement on the continent's perimeter. This feature was less conspicuous south of about latitude 40°S. In part, the massing along the margins reflected the high proportion of overseas immigrants in the population; these tended to concentrate near the ports of entrance. In part, also, it signified the commercial nature of the economic undertakings in which the immigrant population was engaged, a feature which made ready access to tidewater and to overseas markets essential. In some of the more tropical parts it may have been a conscious seeking after altitudinal locations in order to escape the physical discomforts and threat to health associated with the hot, wet lowland climates. Where metallic ores were the principal attraction, it was the continent's mineralized marginal highlands, both those of Brazil and the Andes, which lured the settler. The tropical interior lowlands were relatively empty regions, as were the climatically inhospitable parts poleward of about 40°.

As of about 1650 peoples of European origin in Anglo-America numbered only 50,000 to 80,000, concentrated in a few isolated centers along the Atlantic seaboard and bordering the lower St. Lawrence River.[31] By 1720, when the population of the United States had risen to 475,000, there had been a conspicuous filling in of the gaps, so that seaboard settlement was relatively continuous from tidewater Virginia to southernmost Maine. By about 1780, or the period of the Revolutionary War, the 2,800,000 Americans were still overwhelmingly concentrated east of the Appalachian Highland, although the Blue Ridge itself had been breached in a number of places, and frontier settlements marked the Mohawk Valley, the upper tributaries of the Ohio in western Pennsylvania, the valleys of the Folded Appalachians, and the limestone basins of Kentucky and Tennessee.[32] But the period of phenomenal growth and rapid westward expansion was largely a feature of the nineteenth century, occasioned by high birth rates at home and a flood of Old World immigrants.

Population increased by 32 to 36 percent in each decade from 1790 to 1860, so that by about mid-nineteenth century it had swelled to 23.2 million and two decades later to nearly 40 million. Thus the center of gravity of the country's population, which had been located in the vicinity of Baltimore in 1790, had shifted to western West Virginia by 1850. Including all of Anglo-America, the non-Indian population approximated 25,000,000 by midcentury, with the settlement frontier passing through southern Michigan and Wisconsin, eastern Iowa, western Missouri and Arkansas, and eastern Texas.[33] Here in the eastern and central United States and adjacent parts of Canada had developed the only large and contiguous area of New World European settlement, where in a few parts population densities approached those of Europe.

POPULATION CHANGE SINCE 1850

In the century following 1850 the earth's population is estimated to have doubled; by 1968 it was nearly 2.8 times the mid-nineteenth-century figure, pointing to a further accelerated growth. Simultaneously there were regional differentials in rates of growth so that the modern

[31] Herman R. Friis. A series of Population Maps of the Colonies and the United States, 1625–1790, Geog. Rev., Vol. 30, 1940, pp. 463–470. E. B. Greene and V. D. Harrington, American Population before the Federal Census of 1790, Columbia University Press, New York, 1932. S. H. Sutherland, Population Distribution in Colonial America, Columbia University Press, New York, 1936.

[32] Randall D. Sale and Edwin D. Karn, American Expansion; A Book of Maps, Dorsey Press, Homewood, Ill., 1962, p. 3.

[33] Sale and Karn, American Expansion, p. 15.

world map of population distribution contrasts in some respects from that of 1850. Since the current distribution of the earth's people is the theme of a subsequent chapter, at this point only the more important changes of the past century will be noted here. From Table 2.9 it appears that of the great land subdivisions only Asia did not keep pace with earth's overall accelerated growth, so that its proportion of world population may have shrunk from about 63 percent in 1850 to around 55 percent a century later. This was almost entirely due to the stagnation of China's population growth rate over the last half of the nineteenth century. Africa seems to have just about equalled the average rate of increase for the earth as a whole and so maintained its relative proportion of world population, or between 8 and 9 percent. It was the area of European settlement, on the other hand, that markedly improved its relative position, rising from 28.6 percent of the earth's population in 1850 to 38.9 percent a century later. This improved position was chiefly a consequence of the swelling rates of increase in the Americas (5.8 percent of the earth's population in 1850 to 13.6 percent in 1950), which in turn was based upon rapid natural increase as well as a remarkable in-migration from Europe. In Europe itself (including the U.S.S.R.), which contained 22–23 percent of the earth's people in 1850, the proportion was about the same a century later in 1950 (Fig. 2.3).

Recapitulating, it was a momentous fact that for over 150 years, until about World War I or perhaps a little later, it was the technologically advanced peoples of the earth, with European backgrounds, who had grown most rapidly in numbers. The populations of the less developed parts of the earth lagged behind. But it is equally momentous that over the last few decades there has been a reversal in the positions of the more developed as compared with the less developed regions in population growth rates, and over the period 1950–1968 growth in the latter has been half again as rapid as in the former. This reversal stems from the fact that birth rates have declined in the technologically advanced regions, whereas they have remained high in the traditional societies, where at the same time mortality rates have been markedly lowered. Thus it is the economically poorer, less literate, and predominantly rural populations, chiefly in Latin America, Africa, and Asia, which are now expanding most rapidly, a feature that probably presages political, social, and economic consequences as important as those that followed the more rapidly expanding European population in the preceding century and a half.

REFERENCES

Behm, E., and H. Wagner. *Die Bevölkerung der Erde.* Ergänsungsheft No. 35, *Zu Petermann's Geographischen Mitteilungen,* Justus Perthes, Gotha, 1874.

Bourgeois-Pichat, Jean. *Population Growth and Development.* International Conciliation, Carnegie Endowment for International Peace. January 1966, No. 556.

Carr-Saunders, A. M. *World Population: Past Growth and Present Trends.* Clarendon, Oxford, 1936.

Cipolla, Carlo M. *Economic History of World Population.* Pelican Books, Baltimore, Md. (A537); Penguin Books, Harmondsworth, 1962.

Clarke, John I. *World Population and Food Resources: a Critique.* The Institute of British Geographers, Trans. and Papers, 1968, Publication No. 44, 53–70.

Durand, John D. "The Modern Expansion of World Population," *Proc. Am. Phil. Soc.,* Vol. III, No. 3, June 1967, pp. 133–193.

Fisher, Tadd. *Our Overcrowded World: A Background Book on the Population Crisis.* Parents' Magazine Press, forthcoming.

Haliczer, Josef. "The Population of Europe, 1720, 1820, 1930," *Geography,* Vol. XIX, 1934, pp. 261–273.

Haufe, H. *Die Bevölkerung Europas, Stadt und Land im 19 ten and 20 ten Jahrhundert.,* Junker und Dünnhaupt, Berlin, 1936.

Hauser, Philip M. *Population Perspectives.* Rutgers University Press, New Brunswick, N.J., 1961.

Hauser, Philip M. (ed.). *The Population Dilemma.* Prentice-Hall, Englewood Cliffs, N.J., 1963.

Hauser, Philip M. The Population of the World: Recent Trends and Prospects. In Ronald Freedman (Ed.), *Population: The Vital Revolution.* Aldine, Chicago, 1965. Pp. 15–29.

Huxley, Julian. "World Population," *Scientific American,* Vol. 194, March 1956, pp. 64–76.

Ogilvie, Alan G. *Europe and its Borderlands.* Thomas Nelson and Sons, Edinburgh, 1957. Pp. 230–251.

Ohlin, Goran. Historical Outline of World Population Growth. Paper prepared for United Nations World Population Conference, Belgrade, 1965.

Reinhard, M., and A. Armengaud. *Histoire general de la population mondiale.* Editions Montchrestien, Paris, 1961.

Petersen, William. *Population.* Macmillan, New York, 1961. (The second edition was published while the present volume was in press. G.T.)

Taeuber, Irene. *Future Population Trends and Prospects.* World Population Conference, Belgrade, 1965, Vol. I. New York, United Nations, 1966, p. 191. Document E/Conf.41/2.

The Food-Population Dilemma, Population Bulletin, Vol. XXIV, No. 4, December 1968, pp. 81–99.

Thomlinson, Ralph. *Population Dynamics.* Random House, New York, 1965.

United Nations. *Provisional Report on World Population Prospects as Assessed in 1963.* New York, 1964.

United Nations Population Study No. 17. *The Determinants and Consequences of Population Trends.* New York, 1953.

United Nations Population Study No. 41. *World Population Prospects as Assessed in 1963.* New York, 1964. United Nations Doc. ST/SOA/SER.R/17.

Vavra, Zdenek. "Future Trends in World Population Growth," *Demography,* Vol. 5, No. 2, 1967, pp. 497–514.

Willcox, W. F. Increase in the Population of the Earth and of the Continents since 1650. In W. F. Willcox (ed.), *International Migrations,* Vol. II. National Bureau of Economic Research, New York, 1931. Pp. 33–82.

CHAPTER

3

Contemporary World Distribution and
Density of Population

The concepts of distribution and density as applied to population are not identical, yet they are so closely interrelated that there is good reason to discuss them simultaneously. Population distribution is most often represented by two kinds of maps, one employing dots or points for numerical values, and the other making use of different density categories derived from ratios of number of people to area.[1] Since counts of population are ordinarily available only by civil divisions, it is these that form the basis for most density maps of the chloropleth variety.

Both dot and density maps are relatively simple and unsophisticated, for they involve only numbers of people and disregard their characteristics. Thus they assume men of various cultures and backgrounds are equal in their acquired characteristics, and no account is taken of their great variety of skills, technological levels, physical well being, and educational accomplishments, or of their capacities as producers and consumers. Such maps also disregard the fact that areas of comparable size may vary strikingly in their resource potentials for supporting human life. Most population maps therefore have serious limitations, for they assume a standardization of both people and areas that does not exist.

The dot (or point) map is especially effective in representing details of spatial distribution pattern that ordinarily cannot be picked up on most density maps (Fig. 3.1). Offsetting this advantage, however, is the disadvantage that the dot map is not quantitative—it shows only *relative* degrees of crowding not expressed quantitatively. This the density map does; on the other hand, it is a blunter instrument for showing details of pattern distribution.

By far the most common population density map is the one whose ratio compares total population to total area. This is spoken of as *arithmetic density*. Its weaknesses have already been noted. Its merits

---

[1] Density maps are usually of three types: choropleth, isarithmic, and dasymetric.

72

World Population, 1961

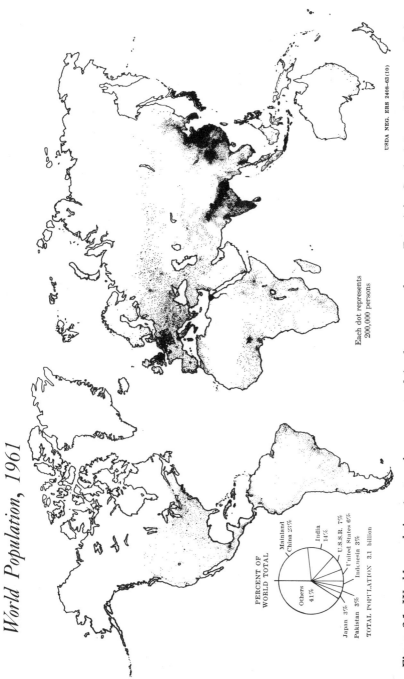

PERCENT OF
WORLD TOTAL

Mainland
China 25%

India
14%

U.S.S.R. 7%

United States 6%

Indonesia 3%

Japan 3%
Pakistan 3%

Others
41%

TOTAL POPULATION 3.1 billion

Each dot represents
200,000 persons

Figure 3.1. World population is strongly concentrated in three great clusters—East Asia, South Asia, and Europe—and in a weaker fourth one in eastern and central Anglo-America. (U.S. Department of Agriculture.)

for showing spatial distribution patterns increase as the size of the statistical areas decrease. A density map of the United States by states has little merit; by minor civil divisions it is far more useful. The almost universal use of arithmetic density reflects the fact that the data required by this ratio are by far the most readily available (Fig. 3.2).

A somewhat more refined form of density is expressed by the ratio *total population/arable area*. This is sometimes called *nutritional density*, or *physiological density*. Here there is eliminated from the denominator all land not fit for tillage. Of course it errs in eliminating all productive nonarable land, including not just waste or barren land but also forest, wild pasture, mining land, and scenic areas. It likewise does not recognize the great variations in the output of various arable lands having different climates, soils, and drainage characteristics. Still, it provides a better indicator than does arithmetic density of the degree of crowding in a region compared with its physical potential for producing food and agricultural raw materials. Japan's arithmetic density in 1960, for example, was 655 per square mile; its nutritional density was an unbelievable 4680, a fact which suggests the necessity for significant imports of food and vegetable raw materials.

Occasionally density maps are compiled by employing the ratio agricultural population/arable land. Here the nonfarmers in the population are eliminated. This ratio is especially useful for indicating a more realistic population density in regions where farm families constitute a large share of the total population.

Certain noteworthy features concerning arithmetic density distributions, on a world scale, may be observed from Fig. 3.2 and Table 3.1. The most conspicuous feature of current population spread is its extreme unevenness. About half the earth's people are crowded onto some 5 percent of the earth's land area. By contrast, some 50–60 percent of the land area probably contains only 5 percent of the earth's inhabitants. Although the ratio of men to area shows a wide range of variability, this is irreducible to any simple formula. An easily recognizable and repeated world pattern, more particularly of the high population densities, does not seem to prevail. Crowded and sparse characteristics are common to traditional societies and to those that are technologically advanced, to white and colored races, to the Old World and the New, and to tropics as well as middle latitudes. Java is an overcrowded island with traditional culture in the wet tropics; Belgium and the Netherlands are high-density states with Western culture, located in middle latitudes; population-saturated Egypt is an agrarian riverine state that developed in an arid environment. Significantly dense populations are lacking in high latitudes. The map shows that the largest areas of high density (>250

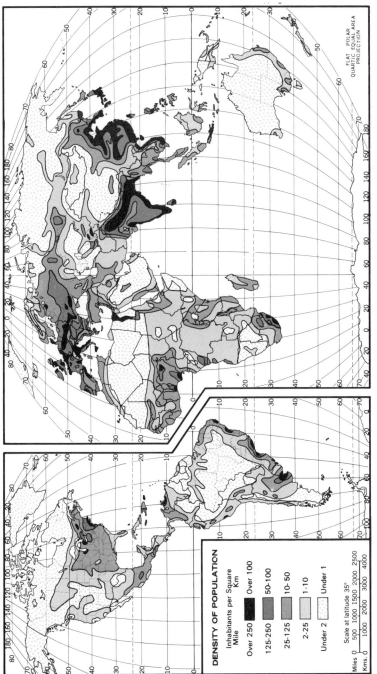
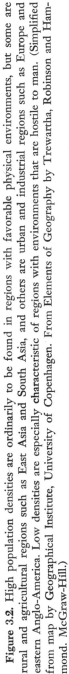

Figure 3.2. High population densities are ordinarily to be found in regions with favorable physical environments, but some are rural and agricultural regions such as East Asia and South Asia, and others are urban and industrial regions such as Europe and eastern Anglo-America. Low densities are especially characteristic of regions with environments that are hostile to man. (Simplified from map by Geographical Institute, University of Copenhagen. From Elements of Geography by Trewartha, Robinson and Hammond. McGraw-Hill.)

TABLE 3.1   Area, Population, and Population Density by Regions of the World in 1960 and 1980 (Medium Variant Estimates)

Regions	Area (Sq. Km.)	Population (Million)		Density Per Sq. Km.	
		1960	1980	1960	1980
More Developed Countries					
Australia and New Zealand	7,973	13	18	1.6	2.2
Temperate South America	4,124	33	46	8	11
Northern America	21,515	199	262	9	12
USSR	22,402	214	278	10	12
Northern Europe	1,636	76	81	46	50
Southern Europe	1,314	117	133	89	101
Eastern Europe	989	97	114	98	115
Western Europe	992	135	152	136	153
Japan	370	93	111	252	300
Less Developed Countries					
Melanesia	539	2.2	3.1	4	6
Middle Africa	6,607	28	41	4	6
Southern Africa	2,670	18	30	7	11
Northern Africa	8,484	66	116	8	14
Tropical South America	13,666	112	210	8	15
Eastern Africa	6,301	75	113	12	18
Western Africa	6,165	86	150	14	24
South West Asia	3,968	59	102	15	26
Middle America	2,512	47	90	19	36
Polynesia and Micronesia	45	0.9	1.7	20	38
South East Asia	4,492	219	364	49	81
East Asia (Mainland region)	11,097	654	850	59	77
Middle South Asia	6,774	587	954	86	133
Caribbean	235	20	32	85	136
Other East Asia	259	47	80	178	297
More Developed Countries	61,315	977	1,195	16	19
Less Developed Countries	73,814	2,021	3,075	27	42
World Total	135,129	2,998	4,332	22	32

SOURCE: U.N., *World Population Prospects*, Chap. 6.

per square mile or 100 per square kilometer) are to be found in eastern and southern Asia, western Europe, and northeastern United States. In some parts of these high-density regions the ratio rises to 500, 1000 per square mile and even higher. In Europe and Anglo-America, both regions of advanced technological culture, high densities are characteristically linked with a strong degree of urbanization. But this is not the case in Asia, where (Japan excepted) on fertile alluvial plains, high densities usually represent predominantly rural farm people.

Very low densities of under 2 per square mile are typical of much more extensive areas than are very high densities. The near-empty lands are largely confined to drought regions, cold high-latitude and high-altitude lands, and some, but by no means all, wet-tropical environments, particularly those in South America. The sparsely populated Anglo-American dry lands are representative of regions with a high Western standard of living; the emptier Amazon Basin symbolizes a primitive agrarian culture.

The present highly irregular spatial distribution and arrangement of the earth's people as revealed in Figs. 3.1 and 3.2 can only be a consequence of the adjustment of population to resources, and to the impact of cultural and demographic influences, over the millenniums of human history. But the present distribution certainly is only a temporary condition, for it is hard to believe that spatial distribution will not change in the future as it has in the past. Just how much and in what ways cannot be predicted. It is probably true that the blocking out of the world in terms of its productive capacity, and hence in a measure its population density, has at present been achieved to a degree not known previously. The discovery of new resources and the development of new technologies for their utilization have today progressed so far that the people of the world are more nearly where they seem to belong than ever before, taking into consideration their cultural level and organization. But that is not to say that a static condition in spatial distribution has been reached. There is no limit, apparently, to terrestrial and extraterrestrial discoveries, and man's inventiveness seemingly has no bounds. Hence the resource base will change as men's ideas change, and, of course, the spatial features of population will too. Over the past few decades amazing new discoveries of mineral resources have occurred, and unbelievable new storehouses of energy have been envisioned in atomic and hydrogen sources. Whether such energy will be used to obliterate population or to multiply it and change its concentrations is problematic.

The factors that affect the spatial aspects of population are as complex and varied as are the patterns of distribution. Three main classes of factors may be recognized:

1. Physical or natural factors, including climate, terrain, water, soils, minerals, as well as space relationships.
2. Cultural factors, embracing social attitudes and institutions, stage of economic development, and political organization.

3. Demographic factors, involving differential birth and death rates and the currents of migration.[2]

Characteristically the factors affecting population distribution do not operate singly, but always in combinations. Consequently, it is nearly impossible to segregate and assess the effects of one single factor. Moreover, it is recognized that the interplay of the various influences is highly complex, and that their effects are brought to bear upon population usually indirectly and through a slow process of adaptation. Probably it is correct to say that *the role of physical factors in spatial distribution of population declines in direct importance as civilization advances in complexity.* As a rule, in simple agrarian societies, primitive and otherwise, where differential population numbers and densities depend very largely on the direct food-producing potentials of the land, physical factors exercise a relatively greater influence. For example, agrarian societies are more subject to the vicissitudes of nature than are technologically advanced urban cultures. Also, the importance of physical factors is somewhat less in modern times than it was earlier, when science and technology were less advanced. In large measure the significance to a population of the natural earth is determined by its culture. Consequently changes in the technological efficiency, aspirations, and objectives of a people require a constant reassessment of the role of the physical resource base.

GROSS PATTERNS OF DISTRIBUTION

A variety of methods can be employed for showing gross features of spatial population arrangement.

Employing the coarsest regional subdivisions, the Old World supports far more of the earth's people (86 percent) in 1969 than the New (14 percent). Eurasia itself contains 76 percent and Asia alone about 56, but all the Americas contain only 14. Less than 15 percent is in the three southern continents.

Great inequalities of population concentration exist within latitude belts as well. Over 90 percent are located north of the equator and less than 10 percent to the south. Within the Northern Hemisphere less than 1 percent live north of parallel 60°; about 30 percent are between 40° and 60°, mainly in Europe; some 50 percent between 20° and 40°, mainly in Asia; and slightly over 10 percent between the equator and

[2] For a treatment of how these various factors operate and interact, see *The Determinants and Consequences of Population Trends,* United Nations Population Study No. 17, New York, 1953, pp. 163–177.

TABLE 3.2   Population by Continents (1966)

	Numbers	Percent
Africa	318	9.5
Northern America	217	6.5
Latin America	253	7.5
Asia	1,868	55.6
Oceania	17.9	0.5
Europe (except U.S.S.R.)	449	13.4
U.S.S.R.	233	7.0
World	3,356	

SOURCE: U.N., *Demographic Yearbook, 1966.*

20°N, chiefly in Asia. About 80 percent dwell between 20° and 60°N, very largely in the Old World.

A further broad generalization is that population is concentrated along the rimlands of the continents; the interiors are emptier. It is estimated that three-quarters of the earth's population dwell within 600 miles of the sea and two-thirds within 300 miles. This feature is a consequence mainly of the dryness of the interiors and their greater inaccessibility.

Reflecting the increasing difficulties associated with exploiting high-altitude environments, population densities and numbers ordinarily decline with altitude. Some 56 percent of the earth's inhabitants dwell below 200 meters (656 feet), but this includes only about 28 percent of the entire land area. Close to four-fifths live below 500 meters (1640 feet). The mean levels of the vertical distribution of population on each of the continents are given in Table 3.3. Mean levels are highest in the tropical continents of South America and Africa.

TABLE 3.3

Region	Meters
Europe	168
Asia	319
Africa	590
North America	430
South America	644
Australia	95

SOURCE: Staszewski, *World Population,* p. 24.

DISTRIBUTION BY ECUMENE AND NONECUMENE

More meaningful, perhaps, as it relates to gross population distribution, is a division of the earth into its permanently inhabited (ecumene) and its uninhabited, intermittently inhabited, or very sparsely inhabited parts (nonecumene). On first thought it may seem a simple matter to differentiate ecumene and nonecumene and represent them on a world map (Fig. 3.3). Actually it is very difficult, for neither the occupied nor the unoccupied land is a compact, continuous surface. In addition, the boundary separating the two is not easy to demarcate. The great ice caps of Antarctica and Greenland represent the more complete and continuous nonecumene. But much of the nonecumene is in the form of isolated unoccupied or intermittently occupied regions of variable size—desert wastes, cold barrens, high mountains, swamps, primeval forest in both tropics and subarctic—which punctuate the ecumene. Hence the boundaries separating ecumene from nonecumene are vague and complex; precise data for many parts are lacking. Even any quantitative assessment of the relative proportions of the earth's land surface that should be classed as occupied is subject to serious error. Of the earth's land area of about 149 million square kilometers, Hassinger estimates that some 27 million (31–32 percent) are barren waste, either cold or dry, and without appreciable human settlement.[3] Large areas within the primeval forest are also population empty, and these and other islands of nonecumene may reduce the ecumene to 80–90 million square kilometers or only 55–60 percent of the total land area.

Even allowing for the dubious accuracy of the preceding figures, it becomes clear that a goodly proportion of the earth's solid surface is largely without permanent human settlement. About four-fifths of the earth's population occupies less than one-fifth of the surface of the continents. Still, the nonecumene is smaller today than ever before, for an established feature of human history has been an ever-expanding ecumene. This has been accelerated during the last few centuries, a period which has seen a spread of European settlement on a scale never before equalled. The expansion of Western peoples many times was not into completely empty areas, but rather a filling in with permanent settlements by a technologically higher culture of regions previously oc-

[3] *Handbuch der geographische Wissenschaft, Allgemeine Geographie,* Zweiter Teil, *Das Leben auf der Erde,* Akademische Verlagsgesellschaft Athenaion M.B.H., Potsdam, 1933. See map opposite p. 192. See also Pierre George, *Geographie de la population,* Paris, 1967, pp. 7–13.

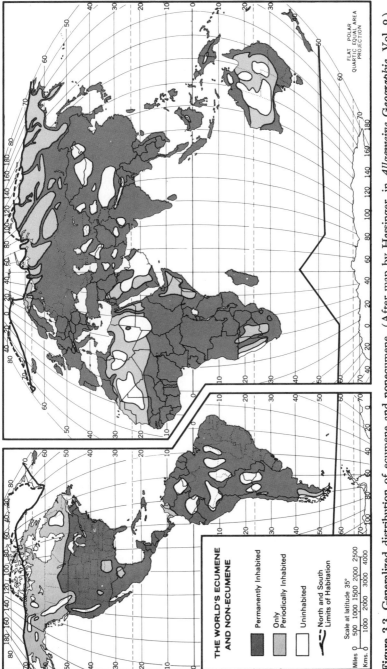

Figure 3.3. Generalized distribution of ecumene and nonecumene. (After map by Hassinger, in *Allgemeine Geographie*, Vol. 9.)

cupied either thinly, or only intermittently, by weaker and less resistant ones. A rapidly shrinking nonecumene is less typical of the present; actually the current settlement frontier is a fluctuating one, advancing in some places and stationary, or even retreating, in others.

In view of the burgeoning world population and the diligent probing for new settlement areas during the past few centuries, it would appear that those lands that still remain empty, or only periodically or very sparsely occupied, must be those that are definitely marginal in resource character and present serious physical obstacles to human settlement. (The only other explanation of the present extensive nonecumene is that people, and especially those of European culture, have been myopic in judging the resource potential of certain environments.) With few exceptions, these obstacles are basically climatic in origin, although drainage, soil, rough terrain, and wild vegetation are often auxiliary factors. In some high cordillera the prevalence of steep slopes admittedly is a deterrent to settlement. But still, it is the highest, and therefore coldest, windiest, and bleakest highlands, that are most empty, suggesting that climate is the main obstacle.

As a generalization further differentiating ecumene and nonecumene, it can be pointed out that the extensive coterminous empty regions are overwhelmingly a consequence of defects in the resource base. Their environments are hostile to man. By contrast, within the ecumene the wide variations in density of settlement are both cultural and physical in origin. Socioeconomic causation is there much more to the forefront. For example, one can scarcely make a good case for the resource base being responsible, even indirectly, for over half of humanity being crowded into the rimlands of eastern and southern Asia, or for another one-fifth's being lodged in Europe.

Lands Hostile to Man—The Nonecumene. Three types of climate —the cold, the dry, and the hot-wet—embrace most of the earth's empty lands (Fig. 3.4). Of these three types, it is those which are deficient in heat that provide the most negative conditions for human settlement. Next in order are the rainfall-deficient dry lands. But where underground or surface water is available in these climatically dry lands, settlement usually is dense. No comparable local temperature exceptions exist in the cold lands. Least hostile to man seem to be the hot-wet lands.

The Cold Lands. It is high latitudes that provide the largest share of the cold nonecumene. Smaller and more discontinuous areas of low temperature exist at high altitudes in all latitudes. Completely without permanent settlement are the extensive ice caps of Antarctica and Greenland and some of the northernmost island tundra lands of both North America and Eurasia. In the still more extensive tundra and forested

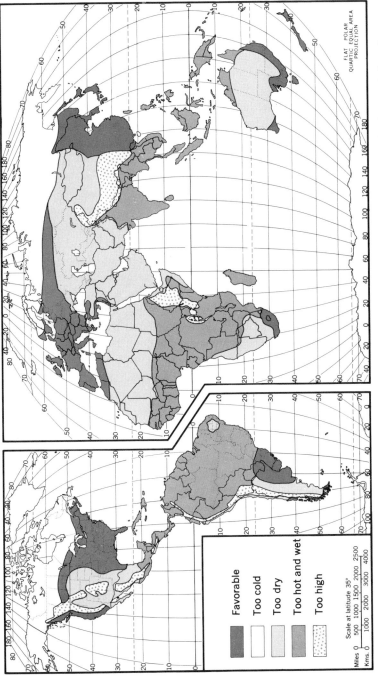
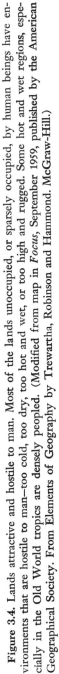

Figure 3.4. Lands attractive and hostile to man. Most of the lands unoccupied, or sparsely occupied, by human beings have environments that are hostile to man—too cold, too dry, too hot and wet, or too high and rugged. Some hot and wet regions, especially in the Old World tropics are densely peopled. (Modified from map in *Focus*, September 1959, published by the American Geographical Society. From Elements of Geography by Trewartha, Robinson and Hammond. McGraw-Hill.)

83

boreal lands on the mainlands of those two continents farther south, some areas are completely without settlement; more are classified as only periodically occupied. Permanent settlement in boreal Eurasia is mainly confined to the river valleys. The Arctic and subarctic cold desert north of about the 65° parallel certainly contains fewer than a million inhabitants.

Chief climatic handicaps in the cold ecumene are a completely absent, or at best very short annual freeze-free interval, a cool summer, and a long annual period without sun. On the ice caps the average temperatures of all months are below freezing, so there is no growing season for plant life. In the tundra, where by arbitrary definition the average temperature for at least one month rises above 32° (but not over 50°), a lowly plant cover consisting of mosses, lichens, sedges, and some bushes provides meager forage for a sparse nomadic-herding population of polar peoples, based mainly on reindeer in Eurasia. In the North American sector the polar peoples are chiefly hunters and fishers. In the boreal climates south of the tundra, where average temperatures for one to three summer months creep above 50°, an extensive forest, predominantly of needle trees, prevails. Only along the southernmost margins of the subarctic forest, and following some of the river valleys in Eurasia, is the summer warm enough and long enough to permit a modest amount of tillage. Fur trading posts, more recently mining and lumbering camps, and infrequent military and scientific establishments occasionally break the monotony of the forest or tundra, but the total aggregate population is small. Auxiliary handicaps associated with the niggardly polar and boreal climates are the extensive development of a permanently frozen subsoil (permafrost), large areas of swamp and bog, a thoroughly leached and poor-texture topsoil, and large regions of ice scour. Inaccessibility adds a further element of discouragement.

Prospects for future important and widespread permanent new settlement in the subarctic and tundra, and a concomitant shrinking of the cold nonecumene, are bleak indeed. It now appears that only isolated islands and strips of durable settlement can be expected, and the cold environment as a whole is likely to remain an ecumene frontier.

The Dry Lands.   On this frontier of the ecumene the great obstacle to durable settlement is an annual deficiency of water in the form of precipitation. Supplementing this is the unreliability of the rainfall, and the sparseness and low utility of the wild-vegetation cover. Desert soils, where they exist, may be high in mineral plant foods, although they are usually coarse, stony, and deficient in organic matter. Within the deserts are extensive isolated regions devoid of population, imbedded within a larger matrix of territory which is only very thinly or periodically occupied by nomadic peoples. This generally empty landscape stands in stark contrast to the dense settlement present in a few oases where a durable supply of surface or underground fresh water is available.

During the past half century or more, application of modern engineering techniques to irrigation projects has resulted in appreciable expansion of settlement within the dry lands. Some of these projects have been expensive multipurpose operations involving not only irrigation but also development of hydroelectric power as well as recreation and navigation facilities. Many times these have been costly projects involving large capital outlays that only a national government could finance. This type of expensive reclaimed land tends to attract mainly high-value crops, for instance, fruits and vegetables. Doubtless the irrigated desert can be somewhat further expanded, but only at high cost, and mainly through the impounding of surface drainage behind huge dams.

Other dry-land reclamation possibilities involve the providing of fresh irrigation water by the desalinization of sea water, and the augmentation of normal rainfall using cloud-seeding techniques. Fresh water produced by desalinization methods, although expensive, is not prohibitively so for municipal use. At present, desalinized water can be produced at a cost of about $65–100 per acre-foot *at the plant*, but this is well in excess of what can be afforded for irrigation water for crops. Still, "there seems to be little question that the market for nuclear desalting will extend into agricultural territory." [4] This will be sometime in the future, and in the beginning will be used in limited quantities only, and for high-value crops only. It is not yet known whether costs can be reduced sufficiently to make desalinized water useful in growing basic food crops.

The costs involved in producing precipitation water by cloud-seeding methods are relatively cheap compared with desalinization. In cloud seeding the question is not so much one of cost, but rather the physical ability to cause appreciable rainfall in dry climates by this method. There are serious limitations, for rainfall can be increased only from clouds that are already raining, or about to rain, and such clouds are scarce indeed in dry climates. There are still no known ways to stimulate useful precipitation from cloudless skies, a condition so common in deserts, or even from clouds too thin to contain much water. The likelihood of utilizing either desalinization or cloud-seeding methods for im-

[4] R. Philip Hammond, "Nuclear Desalting for Agricultural Water," *Nucleonics*, Vol. 23, September 1965, pp. 51–55.

portantly augmenting the water supplies of desert agriculture in the fore-seeable future do not seem bright, but neither are they hopeless.[5]

There are those who believe that despite these obstacles dry lands will eventually be conquered. For example, a Russian scientist [6] points out that spatial distribution of solar radiation at the earth's surface is one of the two greatest determinants of earth resources for human use, since the energy of solar radiation is utilized by the biosphere. Annual solar energy receipts are greatest in the tropical and subtropical dry lands and the savannas. But there a serious shortage of water exists just where solar radiation is at a maximum. Still Pokshishevskii writes, "But humanity is acquiring more and more skill and technical facilities for the redistribution of water, and the control of run-off; thus in the final analysis and in the far future, the zones with most abundant solar radia-tion may be expected to become the richest in the bioenergetic sense, which is specially important for food production. A time may be fore-seen when the present-day deserts and the zones of tropical (but not equatorial) forests will become the main granaries of the earth. . . ." Most agronomists would probably consider this forecast dangerously optimistic.

The semiarid lands surrounding the deserts serve as transition belts between desert and humid climates. They are also transitional between ecumene and nonecumene. Those of middle latitudes have been partially settled by people of Western culture during the last century, so that by far the greater share of the steppe is now under permanent, although relatively thin settlement. In fact, in some areas the dry frontier of tillage moved too far toward the desert, and has been forced to withdraw.

The Hot-Wet Lands. Unlike the other two types of extensive nonecumene, the wet tropics, instead of being plagued with seemingly insuperable climatic deficiencies, are afflicted with a superabundance of climatic energy in the forms of solar radiation, heat, and precipitation. It is the excess of climatic energy and the associated features of a lush, wild vegetation and low-grade soils which appear to have retarded settlement over extensive parts of the wet tropics. Annual receipts of solar energy reach a maximum in the tropical and subtropical latitudes,[7]

---

[5] W. R. Derrick Sewell (ed.), *Human Dimensions of Weather Modification*, University of Chicago, Dept. of Geography Research Paper No. 105, Chicago, Ill., 1966, pp. 31, 65. See also *Weather Modification and Control*, A Report by the Legis-lative Reference Service, Library of Congress, U.S. Government Printing Office, Washington, D.C., 1966.

[6] V. V. Pokshishevskii, The Population and Resources of the World. Paper sub-mitted to a Symposium on the Geography of Population Pressure on the Physical and Social Resources, Pennsylvania State University, Sept. 17–23, 1967.

[7] This does not occur close to the equator, where the abundant cloudiness some-what reduces the solar energy received at the earth's surface.

and in the wet tropics rainfall and heat are both abundant, and the heat is continuous throughout the year. There is no dormant season for vegetation because of cold, and in equatorial latitudes none because of drought, so that the cover of wild vegetation is luxuriant. A dense broad-leaf evergreen forest dominates in those wetter parts lacking a significant dry season; deciduous trees and tall grasses prevail where the rainfall is more seasonal. Nowhere else do plants grow as quickly and luxuriantly as in the wet tropics, and since it is from plants, directly, or indirectly through herbivorous animals, that man derives his food supply, the dense and prolific vegetation is an indicator of a large potential food-producing capacity, capable of supporting large populations.

There are offsetting features, however. Abundant rainfall in the presence of constant heat acts to remove the soil's soluble plant foods so that mature soils are highly deficient in those elements. Under tillage they deteriorate rapidly and need a long fallow period for recuperation. Beneficial soil organisms are scarce. Growth of weedy plants in tilled fields is rapid, tending to suffocate crops not carefully tended. Heat and humidity make for great physical discomfort, hasten spoilage and decomposition, and create an environment stimulating to parasites and bacteria injurious to plants, animals, and men.[8]

Unlike the dry and the cold nonecumene where population is either lacking, exceedingly thin, or only periodic, the humid tropics exhibit all gradations of settlement density, from emptiness to severe crowding. The New World tropics, on the average, are less well peopled than those of the Old World, particularly those of Asia. Just why is not clear. But in both the Eastern and Western Hemisphere tropics there are plenty of examples of both high and low population densities. The vast Amazon Basin is illustrative of the relatively empty tropics, and Java, lowland India, and Puerto Rico of the crowded sections. But the very fact that such variations in density actually do exist clearly indicates that the humid tropics do have potentialities for future settlement probably far in excess of those possessed by either the cold or the dry lands. Kellogg has estimated that 20 percent of the unused tropical lands within the Americas, Madagascar, Borneo, and New Guinea, amounting to nearly 400 million hectares, could be brought into cultivation if suitable land-use systems can be developed.[9] It is in the humid tropics, most likely, that the nonecumene will suffer its greatest shrinkage in the decades to come. The speed of reclamation is another matter.

As noted in an earlier chapter, a frightening aspect of modern popu-

[8] Jen-Hu Chang, "The Agricultural Potential of the Humid Tropics." *Geog. Rev.*, Vol. 57, July 1968, pp. 333–361.

[9] C. E. Kellogg, *Food, Soil and People*, The Manhattan Publishing Co. (with UNESCO), New York, 1950, p. 21.

lation is its soaring rate of growth. A concomitant feature is that this burgeoning is not accompanied by a significant settlement on new lands. Quite the opposite, for the added population is mainly piling up in previously settled areas to create higher densities and greater crowding. This seems to suggest that in terms of man's present productive skills, the contemporary world pattern of ecumene-nonecumene may better reflect the quality of the resource base than it did in earlier periods. Still, one should guard against myopic judgments. In the man-resource relationship both factors are constantly changing. Not only is population dynamic in both numbers and potentialities, but the resource base is as well. The resource base changes with succeeding scientific inventions and discoveries, and with each new plant breeding success. The population optimum in a complex scientific civilization depends not alone on area of crop land, manpower, and loaves of bread, but even more upon the relationship between human intelligence, horsepower, and computers, whose limits certainly have not been reached. So, most likely, the potentialities of the earth for supporting population will change in the future as they have in the past. The new tools constantly being fashioned by science cannot help but modify our present concepts of the man-land relationship.

The Ecumene. As pointed out earlier, great variations in the degree of population concentration exist within the inhabited sections of the earth. Moreover, areal variations in density of settlement within the ecumene, while by no means unrelated to the qualities of the physical environment, are more frequently and more strongly influenced by socioeconomic factors. Thus, whereas the nonecumene appears to be largely physically conditioned, the variety in population density within the ecumene has stronger attachment to cultural causes. Four of the ecumene's main population clusters are particularly noteworthy.

Some 70–75 percent of the earth's population is contained within four primary clusters, two in Asia, one in Europe, and one—the smallest—in Anglo-America. Together the two Asiatic concentrations, one in East Asia and the other in tropical South Asia, account for about 46 percent of the world's inhabitants (this rises to 52–53 percent if intervening Southeast Asia is included). Largest of the four, the cluster in eastern Asia has about 26 percent. Its main political units are China with over 700 million inhabitants, Japan with about 100 million, North and South Korea, and Taiwan. Together India (some 525 million), Pakistan (about 125 million), and Ceylon comprise a great share of the South Asia cluster, whose approximately 675 million people make up about 20 percent of the world's total. The European concentration (roughly 650 million, including European U.S.S.R.) is almost of the same magnitude as that in South Asia. Smallest of all (less than 6 percent) is the cluster in central and eastern Anglo-America, which includes most of the United States' entire 200 million and Canada's 21 million.

Of the ecumene's four main population concentrations, the one in Europe is centered at about 50°N, the one in Anglo-America about 10° closer to the equator, and that in East Asia at about 35°N. Only the cluster in South Asia is distinctly tropical in location. Two of the population concentrations border upon the Atlantic Ocean, one on the Pacific, and one on the Indian.

The four population concentrations pair off in other important respects as well. The Anglo-American concentration, developed as a result of a budding off from Europe, expectedly bears the stamp of European culture, including its distinguishing features of economic development. These two population clusters are far advanced in a scientific, machine-age civilization, individual wealth is relatively great, living standards are high, regional specialization is well developed, and urbanization, the offspring of industry and commerce, is far advanced, with the consequence that urban dwellers make up a large proportion of all the people. The two Atlantic clusters include a great majority of the more developed countries, in which 20 percent of the world's population controls 80 percent of the world's wealth.

By contrast, the premodern world still exists to a large degree in the two Asiatic clusters. Here the people are predominantly poor peasant farmers engaged in intensive subsistence agriculture. Population presses closely upon the food supply; poverty and malnutrition are omnipresent; birth rates are still depressingly high, while death rates, although still high by Western standards, are falling. Consequently, the rate of natural increase in population is large and, of course, in absolute numbers it is tremendous. Urban population comprises a small fraction of the total. Japan is the single political unit within the two Asiatic clusters which has experienced the demographic transition accompanying the Scientific-Industrial Revolution, with the result that it resembles Europe and Anglo-America both in its birth and death rates and in its emphasis on manufacturing and trade.

What is remarkable about the Asiatic population is that it has become so vast and so dense while at the same time remaining overwhelmingly rural. It has not been greatly affected by the processes of industrialization and urbanization to which the large and dense populations in the West can be attributed. This unique situation in Asia has its origin partly in the fact that its intensive agriculture is almost completely oriented toward the vegetable kingdom, and does not significantly involve animal feeding. Such an agriculture in which crops are consumed directly by human beings can support several times more people than a mixed crop-animal type in which much of the crop output is fed to animals, whose products subsequently are consumed by humans. Thus it is the vegetarian diet that has allowed the rural Asians to become so numerous and so dense. Supplementary factors are the great antiquity of Asiatic civilization, its intensive subsistence agriculture, a prevalence of almost universal marriage, and the early age at which marriage takes place.

REFERENCES

Broek, Jan O. M. Climate and Future Settlement. *Yearbook of Agriculture*, U.S. Department of Agriculture, Washington, D.C., 1941. Pp. 227–236.

Chang, Jen-Hu. "The Agricultural Potential of the Humid Tropics," *Geog. Rev.*, Vol. 58, July 1968, pp. 333–361.

Hammond, R. Philip. "Nuclear Desalting for Agricultural Water," *Nucleonics*, Vol. 23, September 1965, pp. 51–55.

Handbuch der geographische Wissenschaft. Allgemeine Geographie, Zweiter Teil, *Das Leben auf der Erde*. Akademische Verlagsgesellschaft Athenaion M.B.H., Potsdam, 1933.

Sewell, W. R. Derrick (ed.). *Human Dimensions of Weather Modification*. University of Chicago, Department of Geography, Research Paper No. 105, Chicago, 1966.

Staszewski, Jozef. *Vertical Distribution of World Population*. Polish Academy of Sciences, Institute of Geography, Geographical Studies No. 14, Warsaw, State Scientific Publishing House, 1957.

Stone, Kirk. "Finnish Fringe of Settlement Zones," *Tijdschrift voor economische en sociale geografie*, Vol. 57, 1966, pp. 222–232.

United Nations. *The Demographic Yearbook*. New York. Published annually.

United Nations Population Study No. 17. *The Determinants and Consequences of Population Trends*. New York, 1953. Pp. 163–177.

United States, Department of the Interior, Bureau of Reclamation. Project Skywater, 1967 Annual Report, Vol. I: Summary, January, 1968.

Woytinsky, W. S., and E. S. Woytinsky. *World Population and Production: Trends and Outlook*. The Twentieth Century Fund, New York, 1953.

Zimmerman, Eric W. *Introduction to World Resources*. Henry L. Hunker, Ed. Harper and Row, New York, 1964. Pp. 1–61, 136–163.

Part 2

POPULATION CHARACTERISTICS: WORLD DISTRIBUTION

In dealing with the spatial distributions and the arrangements on the earth, whether the discussion is of cattle, wheat, coal, people, or any other feature, the concept of numbers—how many—rightly receives great emphasis. But basic as numbers are, this feature needs supplementing by other data having to do with the quality and characteristics of the things enumerated. Distribution of the numbers of cattle on the earth provides a very fundamental map, to be sure. But such a map becomes much more meaningful when supplemented by tabular or graphic information relating to the quality, characteristics, uses, and output of products from these cattle. Whether cattle are primarily for beef, dairy, or draft purposes, and what the amount and value of the products per animal might be, are highly significant characteristics of cattle which importantly supplement an enumeration of their numbers. The same qualifications hold for tons of coal, acres of cotton, or board-feet of lumber.

A similar reasoning applies to human beings. How man uses the earth, the imprint that he makes on its surface, how much he produces or consumes, the nature of his economic, social, and political institutions—the sum total of his accomplishments as expressed in the inclusive term civilization—are all directly related not alone to number of human beings but also to their qualities or characteristics, many important ones culturally induced. The illiterate native of the tropical rainforest whose energy is sapped by debilitating diseases and whose source of work energy is limited to his own muscles cannot create, produce, or consume at the same level as the healthier, educated, scientifically trained European or Anglo-American making use of machines fueled with inanimate power. As an example, the 20–25 percent of the earth's population living in scientifically and technologically advanced nations consumes about 80 percent of the earth's total energy output.

The composition or characteristics of population can be represented by no standard list. But any list of noteworthy population characteristics includes some of *biological* origin (race, color, ethnic stock; fertility, mortality, and health; natural increase; sex ratio; and age structure) and others derived from *culture* (education-literacy, occupation, marital status, rural or urban residence, language, religion, and mobility). They can also be subdivided into *ascribed*, or *assigned*, characteristics, meaning those over which the individual has little or no choice (sex, race, and age, for example), compared with others that are *achieved* and are subject to individual alteration (marital status, education, rural-urban residence, occupation). Many, although not all population characteristics are included in modern census enumerations.

Based upon a variety of characteristics, some of which are described in the following chapters, the world's population has become increasingly polarized into two unlike groups. This dichotomy is one that separates the earth's countries and peoples into less developed and more developed categories. The less developed realm includes those countries (very largely in Africa, Asia, and Latin America) that fail to provide acceptable levels of living for a great share of their populations, with resulting poverty and deprivation. As here used, the term "less developed" refers to economic conditions only; it does not imply cultural retardation. For some of the population characteristics to be described, typologies are developed, and the spatial world distributions of the resulting types are analyzed.

CHAPTER

4

Biological Population Characteristics

RACE

This closely interrelated group of population characteristics (skin color, ethnic group, nativity, nationality), in the minds of many, provides attributes of the highest importance, distinguishing the largest subdivisions of humanity. Race is a biological concept. Yet unfortunately the term has acquired some unscientific and regrettable cultural connotations. One such, sometimes called the "myth of race," and unfortunately widely held among Western peoples, implies that the physical traits distinguishing the different races apart are also indicators of the behavioral and cultural capacities of the individuals possessing such physical traits. Such a belief too often degenerates into the ugly practice of racism. Unquestionably the full gamut of human talents is present in all the principal races of man, and at all social and economic levels. But it has never been established that there exist genetic differences between human subgroups classified according to skin color and other physical traits, which make for unlike patterns of *average* intellectual skills among the races.

Among the biological traits most commonly used to differentiate races, skin color is the one usually emphasized by laymen. But in the scientist's complex and sophisticated classification of race, numerous other physical attributes are considered, among them body height and structure, skull size and shape, facial form, color of eyes, color and texture of hair, and blood type. Since these and other features rarely covary by groups, classification is made unusually difficult. Most of the subclasses lack sharp boundaries, but instead merge gradually into each other. So the U.S. Census adheres to a local definition of race: a person is classified as Negro if he is so considered by his community. Such a person is victimized by the myth of race whether he is a Negro or not.

The notion of pure races is unrealistic, for the earth's population is essentially one of mixtures or mongrels. This makes it nearly impossible

93

to classify races by simple, hard-and-fast criteria. Many anthropologists and ethnographers consider only three primary racial divisions of mankind—Caucasoids, Negroids, and Mongoloids (Fig. 4.1). The white or Caucasoid group is the most numerous and widespread over the earth, amounting to somewhat less than half the human population. It is frequently subdivided into three main ethnic groups: Europeans, Indo-Iranians, and Semites and Hamites. The European subgroup is further fragmented into Nordics, Mediterraneans, and Alpines. The European branch is especially widespread, this being a consequence of European migrations and vast European colonial enterprises. The Indo-Iranian branch, numbering 350–400 million, is very much more concentrated, occupying mainly the northern and eastern parts of Southwest Asia, and the northern and central parts of the Indian subcontinent. The third branch of the Caucasoids, the Semites and Hamites, is largely confined to northern and northeastern Africa (80 million) and the western and southwestern part of Asia Minor (20 million).

Negroid peoples make up perhaps one-tenth of the earth's inhabitants. They are widely distributed. Two branches exist, the African blacks, located both in sub-Saharan Africa and in the Western Hemisphere, and the Asiatic blacks—the Dravidians and Australoids—concentrated in southern India and parts of Southeast Asia and Oceania. The large group of American blacks is mainly a consequence of the slave trade that brought Africans to the New World as laborers on the cotton and sugar plantations.

Yellow and brown Mongoloid peoples, numbering around a billion, make up the third great racial subdivision. The yellow Mongoloids are mainly in East and Central Asia, while the brown Malays and Indonesians of Southeast Asia show the effects of contacts with Australoid peoples.

Although peoples resulting from recent racial mixtures are very numerous, their precise numbers are unknown. The blending of American Indian, white, and Negro strains has produced in Latin America a population which is predominantly mixed in character. White and Negro blends are common in the United States, where they make up a colored 10–11 percent minority, while white and Mongoloid mixtures, called Eurasians, are numerous in parts of Asia. At present there is no conclusive classification of the earth's population, country by country, according to racial or ethnic composition. Distribution patterns of this particular population characteristic on a world scale are less meaningful than would be the proportions and distributions of various racial and ethnic groups within individual countries.

Nationality is ambiguous and hard to define, for it includes such meanings as place of birth, ancestors' place of birth, and citizenship of the

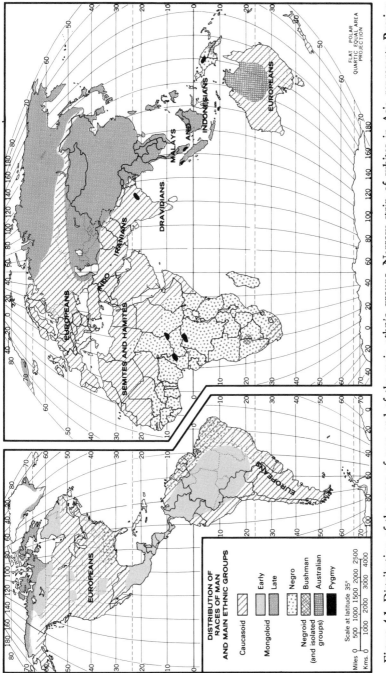
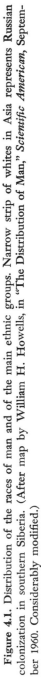

Figure 4.1. Distribution of the races of man and of the main ethnic groups. Narrow strip of whites in Asia represents Russian colonization in southern Siberia. (After map by William H. Howells, in "The Distribution of Man," *Scientific American*, September 1960. Considerably modified.)

95

individual or his ancestors. For population study the greatest value derives from identification of the foreign born, for there often exist fundamental cultural and economic differences between the native born and foreign born in such characteristics as birth rates, death rates, literacy, mobility, and other social indexes.

The physical features that differentiate various races and ethnic groups, noted earlier, do not seem to be of importance in influencing man's culture or the use he makes of his environment. The chief significance of these qualities is not functional for man, either as a producer or a consumer. Ideals of physical perfection vary widely; there are no standards that are universal. It is possible that skin color may have some functional significance in environments characterized by intense sunlight and high temperatures, especially in dry climates. This is scarcely to say that the ethnic composition of a country's population is without important consequence. But the most commonly observed effect of physical characteristics is the generating of unreasonable prejudices which serve to alienate the various racial and ethnic groups within a national population. In the very meaningful separation of the earth's population into its two developmental subdivisions, it is most unfortunate that the peoples with pigmented skins—the blacks, browns, and yellows—make up the poorer and economically less developed majority, and the whites the more developed, affluent, and powerful minority. Thereby may be injected into this concept of a dualism in world population the degrading feature of racism.

DEMOGRAPHIC CHARACTERISTICS

The category of population characteristics called demographic embraces fertility, mortality (including morbidity and health), and the resultant of these two, or rate of natural increase. Like age and sex, these are biological characteristics, albeit they vary widely among different societal groups, for they are culturally influenced to an important degree.

Fertility. *Fertility* is the birth performance of a population as reflected by the number of live births. It differs from *fecundity*, which denotes the physiological ability or potential to reproduce. The former refers to the number of children a woman has actually borne; the latter to the number she is biologically capable of having. Fecundity is a characteristic of individuals and very little is known about the differing biological potentials (if any) of large population groups. Fertility at present is first and foremost "social fertility," for it is largely determined by varied social, economic, and psychological factors. The level of fertility is probably the most acute single indicator of location within a modernization continuum.

Indexes of Fertility. An objective method for determining the level of reproduction of a population is essential. The index most commonly used is the *crude birth rate.* It is the ratio of the number of live births per year per 1000 people (or per 100 if a percentage is preferred). Another index, but one which is less commonly used, is called the *fertility ratio.* This is the ratio of the number of children under 5 years of age per 1000 women of child-bearing age (15 to 44 years). Crude birth rate has the advantage that it is readily calculated and is available annually in those parts of the world that make birth registrations. On the other hand, it has limitations as a fertility index, for it fails to take into consideration the varying age and sex compositions of different populations. Hence it is not a highly refined measurement for comparing the birth performances of different countries and regions. The fertility ratio has the advantage that it is automatically standardized for age and sex composition. It does not depend on annual registration, which is lacking in many countries; it can be calculated instead from ordinary census data on population. Of course, this means that the fertility ratio will not be available for each year, but only those years following a census. And since there is lag of several years in the publication of census returns, ordinarily the latest fertility ratios available may be 5 or more years old.

Determinants of Differential Fertility. Mainly socioeconomic rather than biological factors determine the differences in average family size among present-day populations. Little is known about the effects of fecundity differentials, but certainly they are far less important than social determinants in affecting family size. The average size of a family in the absence of any fertility control is probably between 10 and 15 children.

One important social determinant of family size is birth control. This is purposive action. More numerous are the nonpurposive determinants, of whose indirect operation parents are many times unaware. In Europe, a century or so after the death rate started to fall, the birth rate entered upon a long-term decline. This resulted from the substitution of the business enterprise for the family as the basic producing unit of society. Thus, having children was no longer a necessity; it became a matter of personal choice. Accordingly, the rate of population growth fell off.[1] The social determinants of fertility are numerous, and ordinarily they act not singly or directly but in exceedingly complex ways, whose

[1] Amos H. Hawley, World Urbanization: Trends and Prospects, in Ronald Freedman (ed.), *Population the Vital Revolution,* Doubleday, Garden City. N.Y., p. 76.

operation is often obscure. Normally families are larger in rural societies than in urban ones. They are also of greater size in less developed societies than in the advanced ones. Religious sanctions are an influencing factor, as are social customs relating to marriage, including the proportion of a population that marries, age of marriage, and attitude toward the remarriage of widows. No doubt the economic well-being of a population has its effects upon fertility, but the operation of this factor is far from clear.[2] Other fertility determinants are such population characteristics as degree of education, age structure, and sex composition. And certainly not least in importance at certain times and in particular countries is the influence of government intervention. This may function either to stimulate fertility, as it did in Nazi Germany and Fascist Italy, or it may have the opposite effect as was true in postwar Japan.

It has been long assumed that before conscious control of fertility was practiced, there was no fertility control, and so fertility was high and at nearly the same level everywhere. About 45 births per 1000 per year was usually considered as representative of this stage of uncontrolled fertility. Such is not the case, for social factors such as age of marriage, universality of marriage, and length of marital life are, indirectly, also influential. Other factors involved are the rate of deterioration in the fecundity of women, the frequency of sexual relations, and the mortality rate among married couples. These various factors could cause a range of variation in the uncontrolled crude birth rate as great as 35 to 60 per 1000. This is quite different from the assumed constant rate of about 45 per 1000.[3]

Geography of Fertility and its Trends. Whereas 99 percent of the population in the more developed parts of the world are covered by a satisfactory registration of births, only 10 percent of the less developed peoples are. For about 54 percent of the latter, supplementary useful estimates are available. But for 28 less developed countries, containing 36 percent of the population of the earth's traditional societies, the United Nations found no satisfactory fertility data.[4]

Natality is accepted as one of the best single socioeconomic variables distinguishing the economically less developed realm of Africa, Asia, and Latin America, from the more developed regions settled by peoples of European origin. Present crude birth rates of the earth's countries range from lows of about 15 or a little less per 1000 to highs of 60 or a

[2] *World Fertility*, United Nations Population Bulletin No. 7, New York, 1963, pp. 134-151.

[3] Jean Bourgeois-Pichat. "Social and Biological Determinants of Human Fertility in Non-Industrial Societies." *Proc. Am. Phil. Soc.*, Vol. III, No. 3, June 22, 1967.

[4] U.N., *World Fertility*, 1963, pp. 12-13.

trifle more, and fertility ratios from slightly under 300 to over 1000. But this range is scarcely in the form of a spectrum, for there exists a sharp dichotomy between the high fertility rates of the traditional societies and the low rates of more advanced ones. A crude birth rate of about 30–35 per 1000 is a useful boundary separating the two groups. No authentic less developed country of importance has attained a birth rate under 30; no genuine more developed country has a birth rate over 25. There are few instances of national birth rates between the upper 20s and the upper 30s. The average national crude birth rate in the less developed realm is in the lower 40s; for the more developed countries it is about 20, or roughly half that of the traditional societies. Consequently there is a marked clustering of average national fertilities around a high average in traditional societies, and a similar clustering around a low average in the economically advanced ones (Fig. 4.2). World distribution of fertility is strongly bimodal.[5]

In the typology of fertility here presented, three grades or levels are recognized. The boundaries adopted are 35 and 20 births per 1000. Type 1 has high birth rates of 35 and over. A large majority are over 40. Type 2 has intermediate birth rates of under 35 and over 20. Type 3 has low birth rates of under 20 per 1000 (Fig. 4.3).

Within type 1, representing the traditional societies, the estimated average birth rate is about 40–45; that of Southwest Asia close to 47; South Asia, 43; Southeast Asia, 49; East Asia, 42; Middle and South America, 40 or above (Fig. 4.3). Similar extreme conditions prevail in fertility ratios. High fertility strongly correlates with the following population characteristics: nonwhite, rural residence, agricultural economy, low literacy, usually high but falling death rates, low standards of living, low level of technological development, meager use of mechanical power and machines, and low per capita production and income. Roughly two-thirds to three-quarters of the earth's population is presently reproducing at a high rate. As a result, these peoples are so overwhelmed by large numbers of young dependents that their economic structures are seriously burdened. High birth rate countries are characterized by a squat age pyramid having an exceedingly broad base, to be discussed later. Their peoples in large measure still retain the premodern and early modern feature of a birth rate which approaches the fecundity rate.

Any well documented *trend* in fertility rates within the group of less

[5] Dudley Kirk, Natality in Developing Countries: Recent Trends and Prospects. Paper prepared for a conference on Fertility and Family Planning: a World View, University of Michigan Sesquicentennial Celebration, November 15–17, 1967. Also U.N., *World Fertility*, 1963.

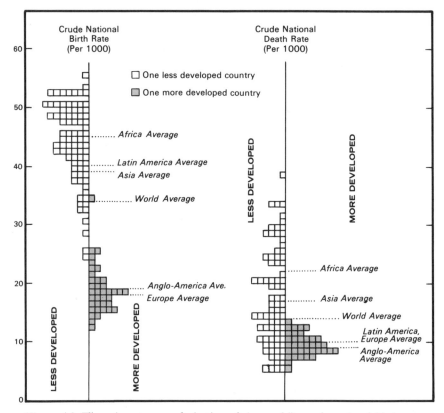

Figure 4.2. There is a strong polarization of the world's crude national birth rates—high in the economically less developed countries and low to moderate in the more affluent ones. Crude national death rates are much less polarized. Low death rates prevail in almost all more developed countries. There is a wide range of death rates in the economically less developed ones. (Data source, World Population Data Sheet—1968.)

developed countries as a whole over the past decade or two is difficult to identify. To be sure, data deficiencies make precise judgments almost impossible. In a few countries the fertility trend appears to have been upward; in a sprinkling of others, mostly small, it has declined. Hence for the vast bulk of the world's less developed peoples there appears as yet no observable upward or downward trend in fertility, but instead a continuation of the high birth rates that have prevailed in the past.

What the birth rate trends within high-fertility countries will be in the foreseeable future is difficult to predict. A degree of optimism derives from the increased effectiveness and dissemination of birth control

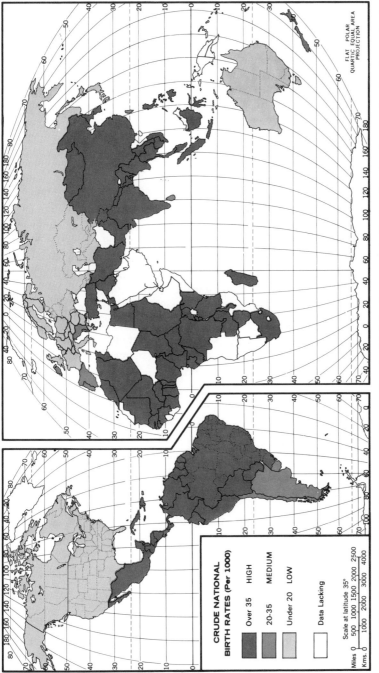

CRUDE NATIONAL BIRTH RATES (Per 1000)

■ Over 35	HIGH
■ 20-35	MEDIUM
■ Under 20	LOW
□ Data Lacking	

Scale at latitude 35°

Miles 0 500 1000 1500 2000 2500
Kms. 0 1000 2000 3000 4000

FLAT POLAR QUARTIC EQUAL AREA PROJECTION

Figure 4.3. Crude national birth rates are rather consistently high in the economically less developed countries, but lower in the more developed ones. (Data sources varied; mainly U.N. Demographic Yearbooks, and World Population Data Sheet—1968, Population Reference Bureau, Washington, D.C.)

101

methods, and also the increased willingness of more and more governments to foster national birth control programs; whether such programs can become operative soon enough to avert catastrophe is problematic. The United Nations' "medium" estimates indicate a probable drop in crude birth rates in the less developed countries from 40+ per 1000 in 1960–1965, to 35 by 1980, and 28 by 1995–2000.[6] Still this accomplishment will scarcely solve their population problems. Some would argue that further death control in high-fertility countries in the absence of birth control is a dubious blessing.

At the opposite extreme of the fertility scale (type 3) are those regions and countries with low birth rates and fertility ratios—usually birth rates under 20 and fertility ratios below 600 (Fig. 4.3). These are the more developed countries, the bulk of whose populations practice birth control. Included in the group with low birth rates is much the greater share of Europe (excluding Spain, Portugal, Ireland, Yugoslavia, and Albania, all but the last being close to qualifying), the U.S.S.R., Australia, the United States, Canada, and Japan. With one outstanding exception, Japan, nations within this low-fertility group are composed of white peoples of European stock. They are generally characterized by relatively high standards of living, an advanced stage of technological development, high educational attainments, large proportions of the population living in cities and engaged there in the secondary and tertiary sectors of the economy.

Fertility trends within this low-birth rate group are variable. In northern and western Europe, control of fertility started from a not-so-high base over a century ago; it has spread widely to these other parts of the earth where people of European stock have taken root. While in recent decades there have been some ups and downs in fertility among individual countries, no conspicuous trends in western and northern Europe are to be observed. This is not the case in other parts of Europe where fertility decline was delayed until recently. There three or four decades ago birth rates were between 20 and 30 per 1000, with some even over 30. But at present, nearly all countries in central, eastern, and Mediterranean Europe have fertility rates on a par with, or only slightly higher than those of western Europe, so decline has been both sharp and rapid. In the 1920s and 1930s the United States, Australia, and Canada exhibited declining birth rates, with the first two dropping below 20 per 1000 during the depression and World War II periods. The United States reached an all-time fertility low of 17.2 in the period 1935–1939.

[6] *Provisional Report on World Population Prospects, as Assessed in 1963*, United Nations, New York, 1964, pp. 310–311.

TABLE 4.1 Crude Live Birth Rates

	1920–1924	1925–1929	1930–1934	1935–1939	1940–1944	1945–1949	1950–1954	1955–1959	1960	1961	1962	1963	1964	1965	1966
United States	22.8	20.1	17.6	17.2	19.9	23.4	24.5	24.6	23.7	23.3	22.4	21.7	21.0	19.4	18.5
Canada	28.1	24.5	22.2	20.4	23.2	27.0	27.7	27.8	26.7	26.0	25.3	24.6	23.5	21.4	19.4
Australia	24.4	21.6	17.6	17.2	19.5	23.1	23.0	22.6	22.4	22.8	22.2	21.6	20.6	19.6	19.3
U.S.S.R.	–	44.4	–	37.6	31.4	–	26.4	25.3	24.9	23.8	22.4	21.2	19.6	18.5	18.2
Japan	35.0	34.0	31.8	29.2	30.1	30.2	23.7	18.2	17.2	16.9	17.1	17.3	17.7	18.6	18.6

SOURCE: *United Nations Demographic Year Books.*

There was a marked rise after the Pacific War, which continued until the late 1950s with highs of 25.0 per 1000 being attained in both 1954 and 1957. Decline again became evident in the last years of the 1950s and has continued down to the present. In slightly varying degrees this same pattern has characterized Canada and Australia. By 1967 the birth rate in the United States had subsided to 18.5, not greatly in excess of what it was in the depression years. The causes for this temporary uptrend in fertility during a period of somewhat over a decade, followed again by a decline such as had prevailed in the earlier decades of this century, are not completely understood.

Soviet Russia represents another trend. In the 1920s, when most Caucasian peoples exhibited relatively low and declining fertility rates, Russia's rate of 40 to 45 resembled those of the less developed countries. It was still high, but declining, during the 1930s, and the decline has continued to the present. In 1965 it was only half what it was in 1935–1939. There was no decade or more of rising fertility after World War II, as was the case in many Western countries.

Japan, like the U.S.S.R., experienced high fertility rates in the 1920s. They were somewhat lower in the 1930s and 1940s, but a sharp decline began in the 1950s, resulting in the 1960s in low birth rates comparable to those in western Europe. This accomplishment, remarkable for a nation with an oriental culture, was a consequence of a conscious and concerted effort on the parts of people and government to reduce family size in an already densely populated country that had suffered serious economic destruction in war.

In intermediate type 2—birth rates between 20 and 35 and birth control rather widely practiced—is a smaller group of 15–20 countries, almost equally divided between the more developed and the less developed categories. They are somewhat marginal in each. Argentina and Uruguay in Latin America; Ireland, Spain, Portugal, Albania, and Yugoslavia in Europe; Israel in Asia; and New Zealand in Oceania—these represent peoples of European origin. In all except Albania fertility rates are in the low 20s and are declining, so very shortly these countries will slip over into type 3. Also included are Cyprus, Lebanon, Ceylon, Singapore, Hong Kong, Taiwan, Barbados, Puerto Rico, and Chile, representing that small minority of less developed countries which has recently experienced a decline in fertility. Their birth rates are characteristically between 25 and 35. Most of these countries are small and insignificant in area and population. Their combined populations represent only 1–2 percent of that of the whole less developed realm.

Mortality (including morbidity and health). Mortality, a more significant cause of changes in population numbers than is migration, is not as important as fertility except in places and years of great catastrophes such as pandemics (in the ancient world), famine, and war. At one time mortality in all countries exceeded that in traditional societies today. Average length of life for the known Western world nearly doubled from prehistoric times to the Middle Ages, after which it remained almost static until the nineteenth century. Rate of mortality decline greatly accelerated in the West during the last 100 to 150 years, in which much briefer time longevity again doubled. The first increase, from about 18 to 35 years, which occurred before the Industrial Revolution, was mainly due to social changes, especially those associated with the consolidation of an extensive territory into a powerful state that was able to maintain law and order. The second, and very recent doubling from about 35 to 75 years reflects chiefly the effects of scientific and technological improvements in agriculture, medicine, and public health. So effective have been the recent medical innovations that startling declines in mortality have been accomplished among the less developed peoples without an associated rise in social and economic well-being.

As a rule, mortality data are somewhat more abundant, continuous, and reliable than are those for fertility. Still, only 14 percent of the earth's less developed populations are covered by satisfactory death registration, and only another 50 percent has it to some degree.

Determinants of Mortality. Expectedly, human longevity and morbidity both have biological and social determinants. Of the biological, food is of particular consequence, for an actual deficiency or serious imbalance in intake will lead to illness and eventually death. But the precise requirements in food for optimum body functioning are controversial. It is a common belief that chronic undernourishment so enfeebles an individual (or a people) that he is less resistant to disease and so dies earlier. But whether susceptibility to disease is directly affected by malnutrition is a disputed question. Indeed, in some affluent societies it may well be true that overeating and obesity contribute importantly to morbidity and death. It seems, however, that in many less developed countries undernourishment and malnutrition are one cause of some sort of enfeeblement.

Diseases, in great variety, are a second biological cause of morbidity and death. Public sanitation and medical science have reduced communicable diseases as a cause of death with startling rapidity. Moreover, specific medications for a variety of diseases, and general antibiotics and anti-infection drugs, have done wonders in delaying mortality.

The two major groups of diseases are infectious diseases and those of a degenerative type associated with the aging process. In spite of the near-miracles performed by medical science and wonder drugs, since man is mortal he experiences a gradual deterioration of the body with increasing years. Where specific infectious diseases are largely under control, as they are in advanced affluent societies, mortality is most commonly related to the diseases of old age or degeneration—senility, vascular lesions, heart diseases, and cancer. In backward societies, where communicable diseases are less controlled, they, plus accidents, cataclysms, and social causes play a larger role in morbidity and death.

Health not only has a negative concept, that is, as a thing that restrains mortality or an absence of disease—it has a positive aspect as well, for it represents a condition approaching complete physical, mental, and social well-being. But health is difficult to recognize and define. Doubtless, average life expectancy is a kind of index of a peoples' health. The ratio of doctors and hospitals to total population is another indirect measure. But these scarcely take into consideration those numerous ailments which, though not lethal, nevertheless cause discomfort, a decline in mental and physical efficiency, or other impairments that reduce the general well-being. The common cold is such an ailment, as are some forms of arthritis. Since health is not readily captured in statistical tables, its world distribution, apart from such indicators as diet, longevity, and specific diseases, is impossible to show on maps.

Genetic factors may be another determinant of mortality, for to some degree, length of life appears to depend upon one's ancestors. But as medical science has advanced, the genetic factor has waned in significance.

Sex differences, too, are a factor, for in all cultures expectation of life is higher among females than males, and the higher the age group, the greater the predominance of females. A part of this mortality differential between men and women is innate and inherent, for the female is less affected by degenerative diseases. There is probably little difference in the susceptibility of the two sexes to communicable diseases; thus as these have increasingly succumbed to medical science, the mortality differential between males and females has increased. Males also have a greater susceptibility to fatal accidents.

Senescence is an unavoidable biological determinant of mortality. The aging process is reflected both in the declining power of self-renewal and in waning ability to reproduce the species. Senescence can be retarded to some degree by medical science, and success along this line may increase. But this "medicated survival" is a mixed blessing, for it means more handicapped survive, more live to be socially and financially dependent, and greater numbers live to suffer from mental illness and chronic ailments. Prolonging life beyond the point where it can be at least moderately enjoyed is of dubious benefit to all concerned.

In addition to the biological determinants of mortality are those of social origin. Among these are social welfare legislation and organizations, public health insurance, public sanitation and medicine, social security, and war.

Differentials in Mortality. That females have a longer life expectancy than males has been mentioned earlier. Obviously, there are mortality differentials by age groups as well. In the poorer societies where modern death control has not been fully established, the age-specific death-rate curve is U-shaped, mortality being high in infancy and early childhood and also in the later years when senescence is a principal factor. In more advanced societies the curve is closer to J-shaped, for there infant mortality has been sharply reduced.[7] Infant mortality (ratio of a year's infant [under one year of age] deaths to the number of live births) is one of the best indexes for gauging the general well-being of a population.

In order to provide readily available, detailed information concerning mortality differentials by age and sex, so-called life tables have been constructed for advanced societies. From these tables can be obtained information of the following kinds:

1. The number of deaths at each age for both sexes.
2. The number of years of life normally to be expected by the survivors at any particular age.
3. The probability of dying during a specific age interval.
4. The number of survivors at each age.

It must be obvious that such life tables provide the fundamental data on which life insurance, one of the world's great business enterprises, is based.

In addition to the biological differentials in mortality previously mentioned, there are others of a social origin. As a general rule such differentials are diminishing in importance. A century or two back, the urban death rate exceeded the rural among Western peoples. This probably reflected the greater crowding among town dwellers, with the attendant dangers from water pollution, lack of sanitation, and infectious and contagious diseases. The rural-urban contrast has now largely disappeared. One might expect that the less affluent classes in a society would have a higher mortality than those at the upper levels. But with increasing control of infectious diseases and improved medical care, the differential existing earlier between rich and poor has markedly shrunk. However, mortality rates continue to differ among employment

[7] Improvement of death control in the United States since 1950 is shown by Figure 10.2, in William Petersen, *Population*, Macmillan, New York, 1961, p. 252.

groups. Generally they are well above average among manual laborers, but below average among professional men, administrators, managers, and farmers. In the United States disabling injuries are highest in the logging industry, mining, saw mills, roofing, sheet-metal work, and construction.

Measures of Mortality. *Crude death rate*, or the number of deaths per 1000 inhabitants in a year, is the index most commonly used partly because it is the most readily available. Its weakness for international comparisons is that it makes no allowance for differential age and sex compositions. Thus the 1965 crude death rates for Mexico, 9.5, and Sweden, 10.1, are very similar, but the apparent similarity becomes less real when one learns that Mexico's population is young, with 44 percent under age 15, whereas the comparable figure for Sweden is only 21 percent.

A somewhat more sophisticated measure of mortality is provided by the *age-specific death rate*, which calculates the mortality rate for each age group in a population. By this index, international comparisons become more meaningful. As noted earlier, age-specific death rates are available in prepared life tables.

World Distribution of Mortality. The current average death rate of the earth's population is believed to be about 14–15 per 1000, or less than half the average birth rate. Although the earth's present average national mortality rates range from over 30 per 1000 in a few countries of Africa down to lows of 5–8 in a larger number of widely distributed nations, the typology here proposed recognizes only two main levels of mortality, with 15 per 1000 as the separation point (Fig. 4.4). Type 1 has high death rates of 15 and over. Type 2 has moderate to low mortality rates of below 15. It has been suggested that there may be a mortality threshold of about 15 per 1000 which must be crossed before a country can be considered fully within the modernizing demographic transition.

Although high mortality predominates in the less developed realm and low mortality in the more developed regions, there is not the same degree of strong clustering of average national mortalities around a high average in traditional societies and around a low average among peoples of European origin, as was true of fertility (Fig. 4.2). World distribution of mortality is less emphatically bimodal.

Type 1, or high average national mortality, belongs exclusively to the less developed part of the world (Fig. 4.4). There continental death rates are highest in Africa (22), next in Asia (17), and lowest in Latin America (10). It should be kept in mind, also, that these relatively high rates prevail in the traditional societies in spite of the large percentage of their people in the young age groups. Their age-specific death rates are

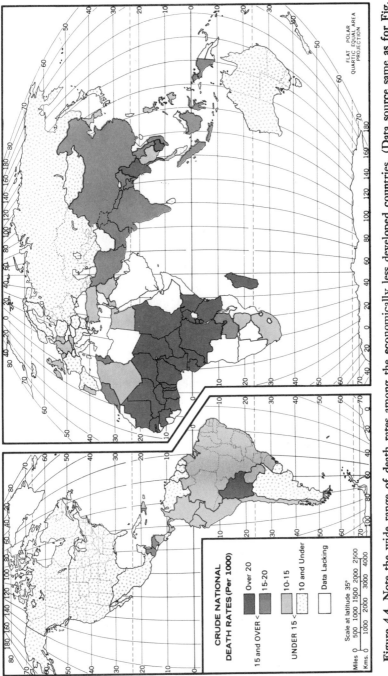

CRUDE NATIONAL
DEATH RATES (Per 1000)

15 and OVER < ■ Over 20
□ 15-20

UNDER 15 < □ 10-15
□ 10 and Under

□ Data Lacking

Scale at latitude 35°
Miles 0   500 1000 1500 2000 2500
Kms. 0   1000 2000 3000   4000

FLAT POLAR
QUARTIC EQUAL AREA
PROJECTION

Figure 4.4. Note the wide range of death rates among the economically less developed countries. (Data source same as for Fig. 4.2.)

109

therefore higher than the crude death rates might indicate. Of the 83 less developed countries with death rate statistics reliable enough to be used in this typology, 46, or over half, classify as type 1. But this division on the basis of countries equates population pygmies and giants. If people are substituted for countries, then about 80 percent of the total population of the 83 less developed countries involved in the typology falls within type 1. But although death rates still continue high among a large proportion of the earth's economically retarded peoples, the less developed realm has shown phenomenal declines in mortality within the past few decades, as Western medicine and sanitation have worked their wonders. Present average death rates are probably only one-half to three-quarters of what they were three or four decades back. Clearly death control has advanced much faster than birth control. High national death rates are much more common in Africa and Asia than they are in Latin America, which has advanced farther in the control of death.

Moderate-to-low death rates (type 2) are characteristic of all of the economically more developed realm, in spite of the fact that the average population age is distinctly higher than in the traditional societies (Fig. 4.4). Surprisingly, 35–40 less developed countries also qualify for inclusion in type 2, but these represent only about 20 percent of the less developed population involved in the mortality typology. Of the three less developed continents, Latin America and Asia are most numerously represented in type 2; Africa is only meagerly so.

Infant mortality rates show much the same world distribution as general mortality. Such data are lacking for much of the less developed world, especially Africa and Asia, but where available the figures are relatively high, whereas they are low for the more affluent nations. In parts of central, eastern, and Mediterranean Europe rates are somewhat higher than elsewhere among the peoples of European culture.

The world distribution pattern of life expectancy at birth, or longevity, closely resembles the reverse of crude death rates and infant mortality patterns described earlier. In much of the affluent, more developed world, excepting two or three relatively unimportant countries in southern and eastern Europe, the life expectancy is between 65 and 70+ years (Fig. 4.5). The range is considerably greater within the less developed realm. Lowest values are characteristic of tropical Africa, where life expectancy at birth is 40 years or less. Over much of the remainder of the realm it varies between 40 and 60 years. In nine less developed countries, divided between Latin America and Asia, the rate exceeds 60 years. Data are lacking for many countries in Africa and Asia.

Natural Increase. Natural rate of population increase represents the differential between crude birth and crude death rates. It differs from

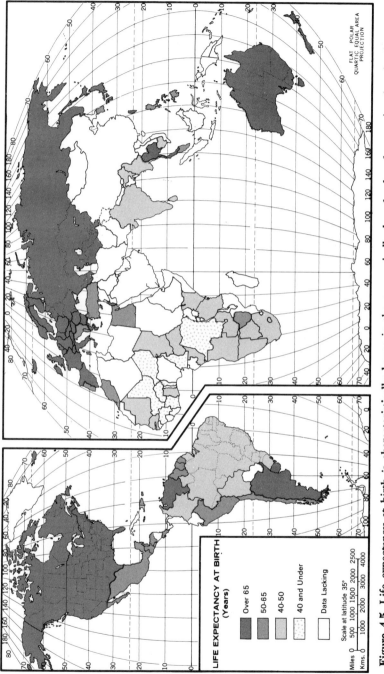

Figure 4.5. Life expectancy at birth is characteristically lower in the economically less developed countries than in the more developed ones. (Data source same as for Fig. 4.4.)

111

rate of increase, which involves net migration (if any) as well. Each year the earth experiences about 120 million births and 50 million deaths. The resultant annual gain of 70 million is the world's natural increase, or about 20 per 1000, or 2 percent, per year. Since natural increase involves two demographic variables, it is possible to obtain quite similar rates of population natural increase from very different demographic structures. For example, a birth rate of 40 per 1000 combined with a death rate of 20 will yield the same natural increase of 20 per 1000 as a birth rate of 30 and a death rate of 10. But whereas the natural growth rate is the same in both cases, there is an important difference between the two involving age composition. This is because declines in fertility are of far greater importance in influencing the fractions of a population falling within different age groups than are declines in mortality. And the differential in age structure will act to create subsequent differences in the growth rates.

In summary, natural increase divides into two general types, one in traditional or less developed parts of the world where growth is rapid (over 15 per 1000, and mostly over 20), the other in more developed parts where the rates are under 15, and in many areas under 10 (Fig. 4.6). Highest average annual rates of natural increase are probably in tropical Latin America (estimated about 3.0 percent), followed by Africa (2.3) and Asia (2.2). Lowest average rate of natural increase (0.7 percent) is in Europe. In seven European countries the rate is 0.5 percent or lower. In only 3 is it over 1.0 percent. In Anglo-America, U.S.S.R., and Australia, the rates are about 1.1 percent.

Demographic Types. It is possible to recapitulate the demographic characteristics (birth rates, death rates, natural increase rates) and at the same time integrate them, by means of the demographic transition model and the typology derived from it, features already introduced in Chap. 2 (pp. 44–50; Figs. 2.4 and 2.6).

In the typology of demographic types presented here and shown in the legend of Fig. 2.6, two main types and four subtypes are recognized. The earth's countries are subsequently typed and their world distributions mapped (Fig. 2.6, p. 49). The boundary used for separating the two main subdivisions is the average national crude birth rate of 35 per 1000. Type 1 with high birth rates of 35 and over is representative of an overwhelming proportion of the earth's economically less developed peoples. Type 2, with lower birth rates (under 35), includes mainly the earth's more developed countries. In addition there is a scattering of small and relatively unimportant less developed countries whose combined populations represent only 1 to 2 percent of the less developed realm's total inhabitants.

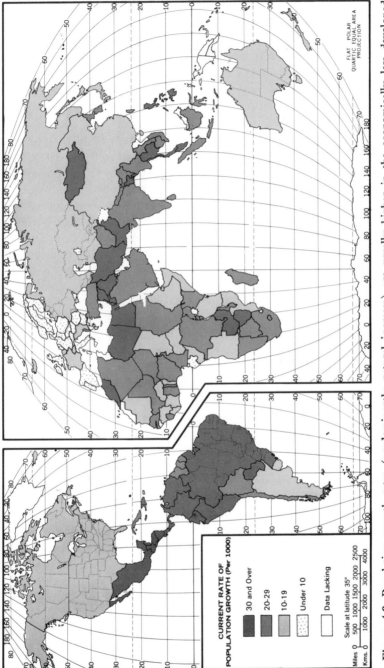

Figure 4.6. Population growth rates (predominantly natural increase) are usually higher in the economically less developed countries than in the more affluent ones. Note a few countries in Africa, where death rates are still high, have only moderate growth rates. (Data source same as for Fig. 4.5.)

CURRENT RATE OF
POPULATION GROWTH (Per 1000)

- 30 and Over
- 20-29
- 10-19
- Under 10
- Data Lacking

Scale at latitude 35°

Miles 0 500 1000 1500 2000 2500
Kms. 0 1000 2000 3000 4000

FLAT   POLAR
QUARTIC EQUAL AREA
PROJECTION

113

Subtype 1a (BR > 35, DR > 15) includes those less developed countries where birth rates are still high and death rates high but falling. Rates of natural increase are for the most part relatively high. The subtype is best represented in Africa and Asia; much less so in Latin America. Subtype 1b (BR > 35, DR < 15) differs from 1a in that death rates have reached a lower level. Natural increase is unusually high. The subtype is especially representative of Latin America, but is to be found in parts of Asia and Africa as well.

Subtypes 2a and 2b are differentiated on the basis of birth rates; the chosen boundary between the two is a birth rate of 20 per 1000. Subtype 2a, where birth rates are still 20 or slightly above, at present includes only a relatively few among the more developed countries. The subtype is bound to disappear shortly as birth rates continue to fall. Natural increase is moderate to small. Subtype 2b, where birth rates are low (under 20), is representative of a great preponderance of the economically more developed world. Here rates of natural increase are low.

SEX RATIO

The sex ratio, or number of males per 100 females in a population, is the most universal measure of sex composition. For the sake of consistency, males represent the numerator and females the denominator of the fraction. At birth, the sex ratio is about 105, for more male than female babies are born. But because infant males have a higher death rate than females, the sex ratio becomes balanced at about 4 years. Beyond that age the proportion of men in the population declines, until at age 95 men are only about half as numerous as women. Sex ratios below 90 or over 110 are considered to be distinctly unbalanced.

Unquestionably the nature of the sex ratio greatly influences the form and tempo of life in any society. It is equally certain that proportions of men and women have a bearing upon marriage, birth, and death rates. Moreover, many economic and social relationships are closely related to the balance or disparity between numbers of males and females. The reckless abandon so characteristic of frontier society may be attributed in part to a plethora of males. Similarly, the staid and religious character of some rural towns and villages may have been influenced by the excess of women, especially widows and elderly spinsters.

Important deviations from a balanced sex ratio originate from demographic and other causes. In the absence of significant migration, demographic causation hinges on birth and death rates. Where both are high, the sex ratio is likely to be fairly in balance. Where both are low, it points to an aging population; here males are likely to be in a minority because of their higher mortality rates, especially at later ages.

Nondemographic influences causing a sex imbalance include such features as migration, war, occupation, and the relative treatment accorded males and females in a particular society. For example, the inferior status of females in many less developed countries combines with the hazards of childbearing in those countries to give higher female death rates and thus higher sex ratios. Long-continued wars occasioning a large loss of life result in a disproportionately high mortality among young males, who bear the brunt of the fighting, and thus also result in a lowered sex ratio. Because migrations are often sex selective, they may function to cause an imbalance between the sexes. Long-distance, especially international and overseas migration is likely to be male selective in its effects. As a rule, therefore, strong in-migration raises the sex ratio, whereas out-migration lowers it by tending to leave behind a concentration of females. For many years Alaska, a region of strong male in-migration, had a sex ratio exceeding 150. Short-distance, internal migrations are variably sex selective, and often depend upon the nature of the employment sought by the migrant. Thus areas dominated by heavy industry, mining, and lumbering attract a disproportionate number of young, unmarried males. Cities specializing in political, commercial, and service functions attract more females.

World patterns of sex ratio distribution by political units are incomplete because of the data deficiencies for so many countries. They are also complicated in origin, for regional sex ratio imbalances usually stem from several causes, some of which act cooperatively and others in opposition. In analyzing Fig. 4.7, it is well to keep in mind that the mean sex ratio for the whole earth is probably slightly unbalanced, lying between 97 and 100.

There are relatively few clearly defined sex ratio patterns of extensive scale. Important differences between the less developed and the more developed realms do not exist. One noteworthy generalization relates to Asia (excluding Asiatic U.S.S.R.) where, with a few exceptions such as Japan, Vietnam, and Indonesia, there is a widespread male predominance. Measured either in terms of area or of numbers of people, Asia has a deficiency of females. The most likely explanation is that in Asia females have a higher mortality rate than males. This in turn stems from the harder lot of women imposed by the cultures of that continent. The same is true for the Arab states of Africa, which, like those of Southwest Asia, show a deficiency of females. Male predominance in Malaya, Ceylon, and Hawaii reflects the attraction which the highly commercialized agriculture of those regions has for young male workers.

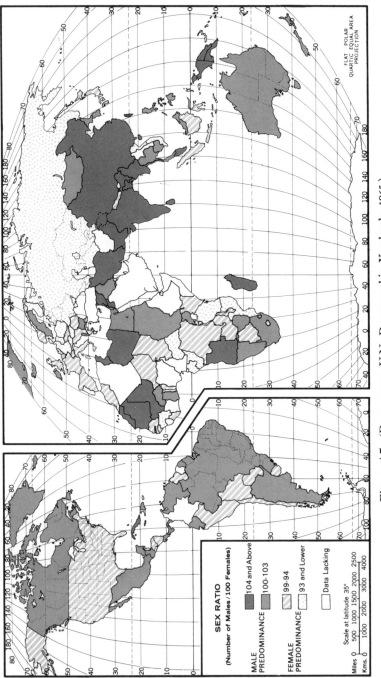

Figure 4.7. (Data source U.N. Demographic Yearbook, 1965.)

SEX RATIO
(Number of Males / 100 Females)

MALE
PREDOMINANCE
104 and Above
100-103

FEMALE
PREDOMINANCE
99-94
93 and Lower

Data Lacking

Scale at latitude 35°

Miles 0   500 1000 1500 2000 2500
Kms. 0 1000   2000   3000   4000

FLAT POLAR
QUARTIC EQUAL AREA
PROJECTION

At the opposite extreme from Asia is much the greater part of Europe (including the U.S.S.R.) where males are in the minority. This is most strongly the case in the U.S.S.R. (82.7 percent) and central and eastern Europe (Germany, 90.4), where losses of young males in World War II were especially serious. The ratios are even markedly lower for those age groups which were in their twenties at the time of World War II. Thus for ages 40 to 44 in 1961 the sex ratio was only 63.3 percent in Soviet Russia and 73.8 percent in West Germany. Less drastic war losses were experienced elsewhere in Europe, so that sex ratios are not so low. In western Europe especially, the prevalence of low birth and death rates points to an aging population in which males are naturally in a minority.

In the British Commonwealth countries of Canada, Australia, New Zealand, and, until recently, South Africa, an important in-migration, male selective in composition, has been responsible for giving to those regions a modest male predominance. It was not until the census of 1950 that the sex ratio of the United States dropped below 100.

AGE STRUCTURE

The age structure, or the proportion of a people contained within various age groups, is one of the most basic characteristics of a population. To an important degree, a person's age influences what he needs, buys, does, and thinks. Consequently the absolute and relative proportions of a population found within the young, middle-aged, and old-age groups are notable determinants of that group's social and economic structure. All aspects of community life—social attitudes, economic activities, political tendencies, military service, mobility, etc.—are affected by the age composition.

Age data have wide use. They are functional to those responsible for planning the educational and military programs of a state. They are vital as well for any efficiently conceived welfare program. The life insurance business is uniquely dependent on age data, and they are essential only in somewhat less degree to large employers of labor, merchandisers, and a host of other organizations, both public and private.

It should be cautioned that since age structure is so closely related to other population characteristics, including birth rate, incidence of migration, and marriage rate, age should be taken into consideration when regional comparisons involving those and other characteristics are made. For example, the crude death rates of the United States (9.5) and Costa Rica (8.5) in 1961 were similarly low. But this scarcely reflects similar health conditions in the two countries, for 9.3 percent of the U.S. population was in the elderly group among whom death rates normally should be high, while the figure for the elderly in Costa Rica was only 2.7 percent. The two countries also differ greatly in their proportions of young people among whom death rates are naturally low: 44.1 percent for Costa Rica and 31.4 percent for the United States.

Determinants of Age Structure.   In the absence of large-scale external migration, and of catastrophes such as war, famine, and pestilence, the age composition of a population is a consequence of its vital rates. The general level of birth rates is the single most important influence on age structure. Thus where birth rates have remained high, even a simultaneous rapid decline in deaths—a situation typical of less developed regions—has led to no significant aging of the population and no marked changes in their age pyramids. This is primarily because the death reduction was spread widely throughout the various age groups. The aging of a population can result from a declining proportion of the young or an increased proportion of the aged. Or both processes may be involved, as in the case of the advanced nations of western Europe where the long-continued decline in mortality rates has been an auxiliary factor in elongating the age pyramids (pp. 120–121). In the economically more developed countries mortality rates are already very low among the young, while medical science is now increasing the proportions of the aged as well, and this no doubt will continue into the future. The social and economic implications of an aging population are tremendous, for as an expanding segment of the inhabitants becomes economically inactive, requirements for schools, hospitals, housing, foodstuffs, pensions, and welfare programs all change.

As noted earlier, high fertility usually leads to a population structure heavily weighted in the young dependent group with relatively fewer oldsters. Low fertility, by contrast, produces a structure in which the proportions of oldsters is relatively high and the youthful relatively few. Europe typifies the latter condition, and Asia, Africa, and Latin America the former.

Migration often affects the age structure, and hence the profiles of the age-sex pyramid, because migrations are likely to be age as well as sex selective. The extent to which males and females of various ages are involved in population shifts depends on the nature and distance of the migration. Sex selectivity in migration will be commented on in a later section. Almost all kinds of migration involve young adults more than the other age groups. Consequently the country or locality of strong out-migration is likely to show a diminished proportion in the age groups of 20–25 to 45. Regions of in-migration may show various degrees of excess of these same young adults.

The Age Pyramid. The usual procedure for graphically representing age structure in a population is through the construction of what is called an age pyramid (Fig. 4.8). In it the vertical dimension is typically graduated in groups of years, usually 5, beginning with 0 at the base, and up to 80 or 90 at the top. The horizontal axis shows the percentages of males (left of vertical axis) and females (right of axis) within the age groups. Under normal conditions the number of people at each year of age will be fewer than for the preceding year. It is for this reason that the age structure of a population graphically represented tends to take the shape of a pyramid. A high degree of symmetry is usually not present, for the ratio of males to females differs from one age group to another. This is especially true in the higher age groups where elderly females predominate. Irregularities and some asymmetries in the pyramid profile reflect historical events—wars, epidemics, famines, depressions, "baby booms"—peculiar to a particular country. Severe military losses suffered by young males in war create a marked indentation in such a pyramid. They reduce the size of the younger age groups as well, since the young men who died could not sire the children they otherwise would have. Such scars are especially conspicuous on the age pyramids of Soviet Russia, Germany, and France. The severe economic depression of the 1930s, also tended to reduce the birth rate, leaving a marked indentation on the pyramids of many Western countries including the United States.

Two general population-pyramid shapes exist: (1) the squat triangular profile with a broad base, reflecting a young population, and (2) an elongated profile, approaching more closely the shape of a rectangle, with a narrow base, typical of an old population. The elongated profile is typified by the countries of western Europe where fertility and mortality rates are both low. The broad-base pyramid exemplifies most of the less developed countries where fertility is high and mortality relatively so, but falling. But in addition to the two general pyramid types there is a great variety of intermediate and modified shapes reflecting the different population histories of individual countries. Where fertility and mortality rates remain unchanged the pyramid is static in shape. Each step in the pyramid differs from the one below only by the number of deaths in that age group. If the number of births increases from year to year the pyramid continues to broaden at the base. Decline in number of births causes the pyramid to draw in at the base—like a light bulb. Such was the shape of the pyramid for the United States in 1940.

Age Groups. Because of the unusual importance of age structure,

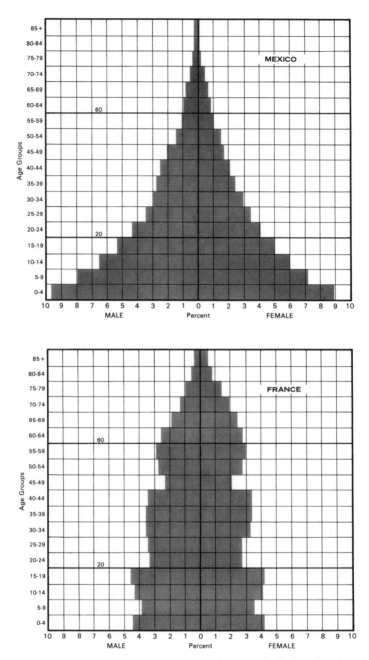

Figure 4.8. The representative age pyramid of economically less developed countries has a broad base and a narrow tip. This reflects a situation in which there is a large percentage of children, and a small percentage of oldsters, in the population

120

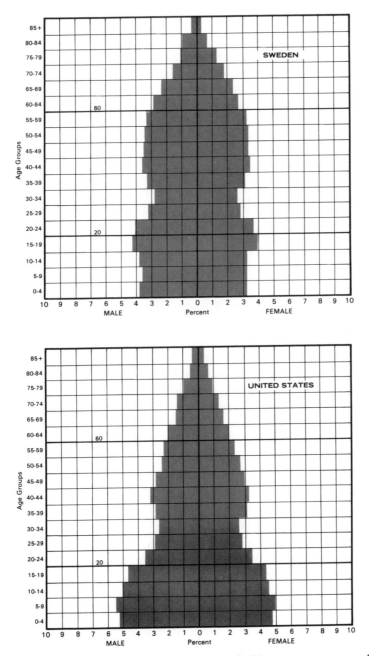

(see Mexico). Children are proportionately fewer and oldsters more numerous in the more affluent countries, resulting in an age pyramid with a squarer shape.

this characteristic is commonly used as a base for comparing the populations of different countries and regions. To simplify the procedure, populations usually are divided into uniform age groups. These may be few or many, depending upon the needs, but a very common subdivision is into three basic groups: young, adult, and aged. The boundaries between these groups are not completely standardized, but the young are normally considered to be under 15, or possibly 20, the aged 65 and over, and adults between these two.

The youthful group is proportionately large in economically less advanced societies where the birth rate is high. Hence a young age structure must be characteristic of a large share of the earth's population, probably as much as three-quarters. Significantly, this large youthful population represents, for the most part, an economically unproductive segment. Yet it is an expensive segment, for it must be fed, clothed, housed, and educated, and hence represents a serious economic burden for the poorer, less developed countries. There too an abundance of young lives also assures a suffocatingly high birth rate in the near future.

The aged group is proportionally larger in the economically more advanced societies, where the young group shrinks. Among the aged there is usually a strong majority of females and widows. Like the young, old people represent for the most part an economically unproductive group. It is this group for which large public expenditure must be made to cover the cost of welfare programs, including medical and hospital care, as well as general social security. It may be reemphasized at this point that the main factor in the aging of a population is decline in fertility rather than in mortality. It must be obvious, though, that aging can come about both through an increasing proportion of oldsters and a declining proportion of youngsters. Regional variations in population structure are mainly to be observed in the proportions of the two dependent groups, the young and the old. These tend to be in inverse relationship unless migration upsets the proportions.

The adult group—the economically most productive, biologically most reproductive, and most mobile of the three—normally supports a large percentage of the other two. Expectedly the proportion of a population classed as adult varies less from one country to another than do the other two. But generally the proportions are highest in the advanced countries and lowest in the underdeveloped ones. The great majority of national populations are preponderantly in the adult and young age groups. Few countries have a large proportion of oldsters and these are mainly in Europe. The social and economic effects of the varying proportions of national populations falling within these three age groups,

TABLE 4.2   Population in Different Age Groups for Selected Countries
(about 1960, percent)

	Young (under 15)	Adult (15–64)	Aged (65 and over)	Young + Aged	Young + Aged / Adults
More Developed					
Sweden	21.9	66.2	11.9	33.8	51.2
United States	31.4	59.3	9.3	40.7	68.6
France	25.4	62.5	12.1	37.5	60.1
Less Developed					
Brazil	42.3	55.0	2.7	45.0	81.8
Philippines	45.7	51.6	2.7	48.4	93.8
Ghana	44.5	52.3	3.2	47.7	91.2

SOURCE: *United Nations Demographic Yearbooks.*

and the geographical distribution of these variations, are of the greatest importance.

Age Indexes.   Various ratios involving the three main age groups form several significant age indexes. The number of possible ratios is considerable. Among them are the following:

$$\frac{aged}{young}, \quad \frac{aged}{adults}, \quad \frac{aged}{young + adults}, \quad \frac{young}{adults},$$

$$\frac{young}{aged}, \quad \frac{young}{aged + adults}, \quad \frac{young + aged}{adults}.$$

These indexes function to separate the earth's countries into rational groups. The last of those listed above, one of the most important, is known as the *dependency ratio.* It compares the proportion of a population which is in the relatively nonproductive ages, under 20 (or 15) and over 65, with those of working age, 20 to 64. Thus the dependency ratio is in the nature of an index representing the age-produced drain on a country's manpower resources. Numerous countries have high dependency ratios mainly because of the large proportion of young; a smaller number are burdened with many oldsters. From the data in Table 4.2 for a few representative advanced and underdeveloped countries, what stands out is that the dependency ratio is distinctly higher in the poorer countries than in the richer, more advanced ones. Unfortunately it is those states economically least able to stand the drain that have the largest proportions of dependents. In their case the dependents are mainly children. As an example, 54 percent of Mexico's population is under 20. In the wealthy countries, in contrast, a relatively larger proportion of the dependent group is oldsters. The dependency ratio for the United States, one of the most affluent of the more developed nations, seems high. This reflects mainly its higher birth rates over a period of 15 years or so following World War II, and hence the higher proportion of children in the United States than in the European countries. Table 4.3 shows that in the United States the proportion of those over 65 has constantly increased over the past 140 years while the proportion under 20 continued to decline until the last decade or two, when fertility, for a short time, shot up rapidly. The dependency ratio therefore fell, and the working-force ratio rose, until about 1940, after which the situation was reversed. Obviously the dependency ratio of a society must greatly influence the proportion of the national income going into savings, investment, pensions, welfare, and education. In reverse, it reflects the percentage of the population that is active in creating the wealth. The young and old groups, although both composed mainly of dependents, require expenditures for somewhat different purposes.

World Patterns of Age Structure. There are several ways for showing graphically the variations in age structure among the countries of the earth. One method is to draw age pyramids for many, or at least representative, countries on a world map. This provides a visual impression, to be sure, but it lacks precision. Another method is to show, country by country, the proportions of the young and the aged in the total population. On Fig. 4.9, which shows the proportions of children under 15 years of age, three groupings are conspicuous. It is almost exclusively the high-birth rate, less developed regions—Africa, Asia, and Latin America—that have high percentages of over 40. To be sure, the map reveals large national data gaps in all three continents, but supplementary information indicates that these countries also belong in the high group. At the other extreme is most of western, central, and Mediterranean

TABLE 4.3   Age Distribution in the United States (percent)

	1820	1860	1900	1940	1950	1960
Under 20—preworking force	58	51	44	34	34	39
20–64—working force	40	46	52	59	58	52
Over 65—retired	2	3	4	7	8	9

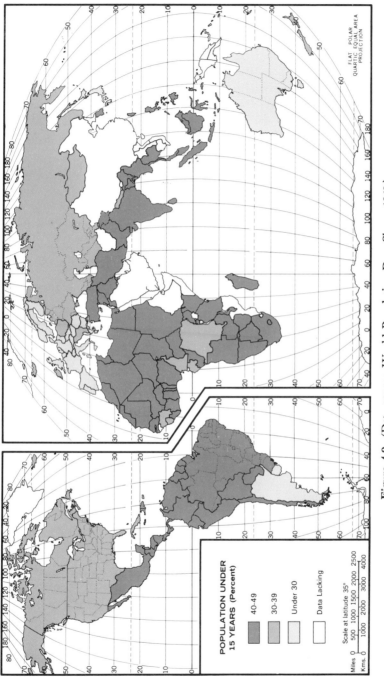

Figure 4.9. (Data source World Population Data Sheet—1968.)

125

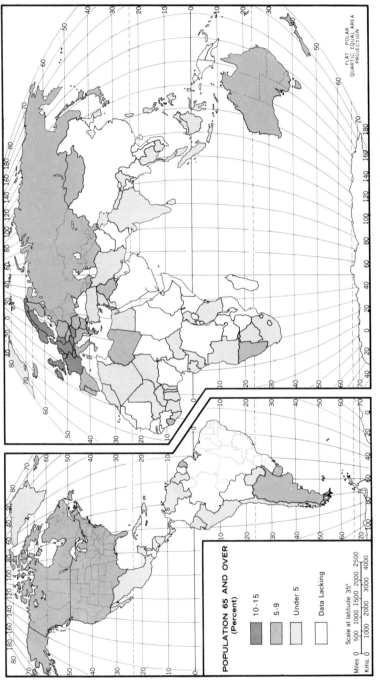

POPULATION 65 AND OVER
(Percent)

- 10-15
- 5-9
- Under 5
- Data Lacking

Scale at latitude 35°

Miles 0   500 1000 1500 2000 2500
Kms. 0 1000 2000 3000 4000

FLAT POLAR
QUARTIC EQUAL AREA
PROJECTION

Figure 4.10. (Data source U.N. Demographic Yearbook, 1965.)

Europe where the percentage of children is small, typically under 30. Here, especially in western Europe, birth rates have been low for some time. Recently Japan has also slipped into this group with relatively few children; also Australia and Argentina. Then there is an intermediate group, with proportions between 30 and 39, which includes the United States, the U.S.S.R., Canada, and New Zealand. They are a part of the European culture area, and characterized by high standards of living, but their birth rates have been somewhat higher than those of the heartland. Still, the trend is downward, so that the time is not far distant when they too will fall within the group where the percentage of the young is under 30.

Figure 4.10, showing the proportions of total population in the aged group (65 and over), is almost Fig. 4.9 in reverse. Again three groups of countries are recognized. A small proportion of oldsters is generally characteristic of the less developed or poor countries in Africa, Latin America, and Asia. National data gaps are again very numerous, but it is believed that nearly all countries for which data are lacking would repeat the above pattern. At the other extreme are western Europe and part of central Europe where the relative numbers of the aged are great (over 10 percent). Mediterranean Europe is not included. Intermediate in character is a third group with proportions falling between 5 and 9 percent inclusive. It is composed of nearly the same group of countries that made up the intermediate group as applied to young people—Anglo-America, the U.S.S.R., New Zealand, and Japan. In addition, most of Mediterranean Europe, Australia and Argentina are included.

REFERENCES

Race

Boyd, W. C., and I. Asimov. *Races and Peoples.* Abelard-Schuman, New York, 1955.

Broek, Jan O. M., and John W. Webb. *A Geography of Mankind.* McGraw-Hill, New York, 1968. Pp. 73–95.

Clarke, John I. *Population Geography.* Pergamon Press, Oxford, 1965. Pp. 93–96.

Dobzhansky, Theodosius. "The Present Evolution of Man," *Scientific American,* Vol. 203, September 1960, pp. 206–208.

George, Pierre. *Géographie de la Population.* Presses Universitaires de France, Paris, 1967. Pp. 41–48.

Howells, Wm. W. *Mankind in the Making.* Doubleday, Garden City, N.Y., 1959.

Howells, Wm. W. "The Distribution of Man," *Scientific American,* Vol. 203, September 1960, pp. 112–120.

Montagu, Ashley. *Man's Most Dangerous Myth: The Fallacy of Race.* New York, 1942; 4th ed., Cleveland, 1964.

Montagu, Ashley. *The Myth of Race.* Vista, United Nations Association, September–October 1967. Pp. 36–42.

Petersen, William. *Population.* Macmillan, New York, 1961. Pp. 114–152 (2nd ed. 1969).

Schwidetsky, I. *Die neue Rassenkunde.* G. Fischer, Stuttgart, 1962.

Smith, T. Lynn. *Fundamentals of Population Study.* Lippincott, Philadelphia, Pa., 1960. Pp. 109–147.

Tax, S. (ed.). *The Evolution of Man: Man, Culture and Society.* University of Chicago Press, Chicago, 1960.

Thomlinson, Ralph. *Population Dynamics.* Random House, New York, 1965. Pp. 439–449.

Demographic Characteristics

Beaujeu-Garnier, J. *Geography of Population.* St. Martin's Press, New York, 1966. Pp. 85–166.

Bourgeois-Pichat, Jean. "Social and Biological Determinants of Human Fertility in Nonindustrial Societies," *Population Problems, Proc. Am. Phil. Soc.,* Vol. III, No. 3, June 22, 1967, pp. 160–163.

Coale, Ansley J. "The Voluntary Control of Human Fertility," *Population Problems, Proc. Am. Phil. Soc.,* Vol. III, No. 3, June 22, 1967, pp. 164–169.

Kirk, Dudley. Natality in Developing Countries. Paper read at Fertility and Family Planning; A World View, University of Michigan Sesquicentennial Celebration, Ann Arbor, Nov. 15–17, 1967.

Kiser, C. V., and P. K. Whelpton. "Social and Psychological Factors Affecting Fertility," *Milbank Memorial Fund Quarterly,* Vol. 36, 1958, pp. 282–329.

Petersen, William. *Population.* Macmillan, New York, 1961. Pp. 209–271 (2nd ed. 1969).

Progress and Problems of Fertility Control Around the World. Demography (Special Issue), Vol. 5, No. 2, 1969.

Ryder, Norman B. "The Character of Modern Fertility," *Ann. Am. Acad. Polit. and Soc. Sci.,* Jan., 1967, pp. 26–36. (Special issue: *World Population,* John W. Durand, ed.)

Smith, T. E. "The Control of Mortality," *Ann. Am. Acad. Polit. and Soc. Sci.,* Jan., 1967, pp. 16–25. (Special issue: *World Population,* John W. Durand, ed.)

Smith, T. Lynn. *Fundamentals of Population Study.* Lippincott, Philadelphia, Pa., 1960. Pp. 271–414.

Stamp, L. Dudley. *The Geography of Life and Death.* Collins, The Fontana Library, London, 1964.

Stockwell, Edward G. *Population and People.* Quadrangle Books, Chicago, 1968. Pp. 24–124.

Stolnitz, George J. The Demographic Transition: From High to Low Birth Rates. In Ronald Freedman (ed.), *Population: The Vital Revolution.* Doubleday, Garden City, N.Y., 1964. Pp. 30–46.

Thomlinson, Ralph. *Population Dynamics.* Random House, New York. 1965. Chaps. 9–10, pp. 73–209.

United Nations. *Report on the World Social Situation, 1957.* New York, 1957. Health Conditions, pp. 28–48; Food and Nutrition, pp. 49–63.

United Nations Population Bulletin No. 6. *World Mortality.* New York, 1963. United Nations Population Bulletin No. 7. *World Fertility.* New York, 1963.

Wrong, Dennis H. *Population and Society.* Random House, New York, 1961. Chaps. 4 and 5, pp. 49–83.

Sex Composition

Clarke, John I. *Population Geography.* Pergamon, Oxford, 1965. Pp. 71–76.

Petersen, William. *Population.* Macmillan, New York, 1961. Pp. 69–85 (2nd ed. 1969).

Smith, T. Lynn. *Fundamentals of Population Study.* Lippincott, Philadelphia, Pa., 1960. Pp. 181–211.

Thomlinson, Ralph. *Population Dynamics.* Random House, New York, 1965. Pp. 428–431.

Age Composition

Clarke, John I. *Population Geography.* Pergamon, Oxford, 1965. Pp. 63–71.

Coale, Ansley J. How a Population Ages or Grows Younger, in Ronald Freedman (ed.), *Population: The Vital Revolution.* Doubleday, Garden City, N.Y., 1964. Pp. 47–58.

Petersen, William. *Population.* Macmillan, New York, 1961. Pp. 69–85 (2nd ed. 1969).

Smith, T. Lynn. *Fundamentals of Population Study.* Lippincott, Philadelphia, Pa., 1960. Pp. 148–180.

Spengler, Joseph J. "Aging Populations: Mechanics, Historical Emergence, Impact," *Law and Contemporary Problems,* Vol. 27, I, 1962, pp. 2–21.

Thomlinson, Ralph. *Population Dynamics.* Random House, New York, 1965. Pp. 428–439.

United Nations Population Study No. 26. *The Aging of Populations and its Economic and Social Implications.* New York, 1956.

Zelinsky, Wilbur. "Toward a Geography of the Aged," *Geog. Rev.,* Vol. 56, July 1966, pp. 445–447.

CHAPTER

5

Cultural Population Characteristics

MARITAL STATUS

Marital status refers to the proportions of a population that are single, married, widowed, or divorced. Not only is an individual's personal happiness strongly dependent upon his marital condition, but the well-being of any society is conditioned by the proportions of its people falling within the several marital groups. Among the useful items of information related to marital status are the median age of the first marriage and the divorce rates. The former, of course, affects the length of the reproductive period, and hence the birth rate.

The married state among adults is preeminent among both sexes, and monogamy is the most universal form of marriage. Absolute monogamy is at present legally enforced in the Western world, but polygamy was accepted by both state and church as late as the mid-seventeenth century.

The median age at the time of first marriage differs with time and also geographically. In the United States, it has shown a long-term decline, and by 1961 was down to 22.8 years for men and 20.2 for women. American families are completing reproduction at an earlier age than formerly, with the result that women can enter the labor force in greater numbers. Obviously, marriage becomes less of a financial problem for the male if his wife can work.

Even though marriage conditions vary widely over the earth, it is difficult to make comparisons which involve worldwide patterns. In part, this stems from a lack of data for many countries. Also, marital status depends greatly on age structure, which in turn varies between countries. So unless age structure is taken into consideration, a comparison of marital conditions between countries is not too meaningful. Only a few broad generalizations will be noted here.

Comparing the two profiles representing the relationship of age to marital status by sexes, universally the one for females reaches its maximum at an earlier age than that for males. With only a very few exceptions, the figures at the height of the profiles representing the proportions of married men and women in the population is higher for males than for females.

A tendency to marry at the earliest ages is most pronounced in the less developed realm, although, to be sure, data on this characteristic are lacking for many individual countries. A postponement of marriage to later years is especially characteristic of certain countries in western and central Europe.

Marriage is most universal in India, Ceylon, Japan, and Egypt. Least likely to contract formal marriage arrangements are the Latin Americans, although common-law marriage is widespread, and children born out of wedlock are very numerous.

EDUCATION AND LITERACY

Educational attainment ranks high in importance among the various qualities of a population. Obviously, only an informed and educated citizenry can make intelligent use of the ballot in a democratic society. Moreover, a low degree of literacy and a lack of adequate training are serious obstacles to economic improvement in nearly all traditional societies. One of the best measurements of the extent to which a people is investing in the future is the effort and money spent on education.

Seemingly the number of years of formal schooling would be one of the best indexes of a population's educational attainment. Such data are now provided for the more advanced countries by their censuses, but they are still lacking for much of Africa, Asia, and Latin America. Moreover, on a world basis, data on years of schooling do not provide a highly valid measurement of comparative educational accomplishments, for duration of the school year and the standards of work are highly variable between countries.

The most basic minimum measurement of educational status is the degree of literacy. But even that is difficult to determine, for what is needed is a rough indicator of ability to use written materials. As a matter of convenience, literacy is usually defined as the ability to read and write one's name in the language of a country. This makes the qualification less meaningful, for close to 100 percent of the population in the most advanced nations is literate by this low standard.

World Patterns. The tempo of increase in world literacy has accelerated in recent decades. As late as 1930 only about 40 percent of the earth's population was estimated to be literate, by 1955 the figure

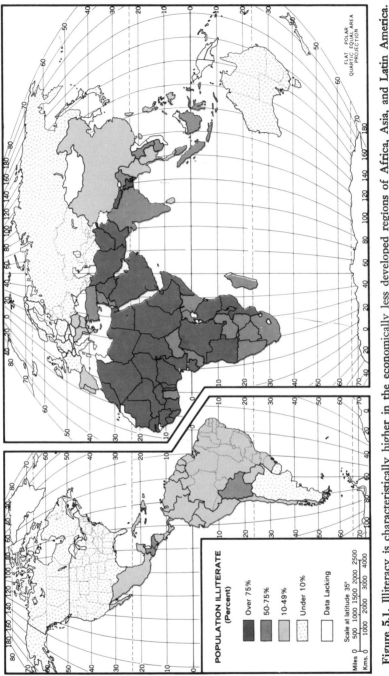

Figure 5.1. Illiteracy is characteristically higher in the economically less developed regions of Africa, Asia, and Latin America. Still, the range of illiteracy is large among the less developed continents and countries. (Data source same as for Fig. 4.9.)

132

probably had risen to 50 percent, and it may be close to 60 percent at present.

Regional variations in literacy are striking, the principal dichotomy being between the economically less developed and the more developed realms. The percentages of illiterates of the total 15 years and older population of a country are shown in Fig. 5.1. In Anglo-America, western Europe, U.S.S.R., Australia, New Zealand, and Japan less than 5 percent of the population is illiterate. Highest among the European peoples are some of the countries of eastern and southern Europe where in several instances average illiteracy rises to over 20 percent. Over the greater share of Africa, educationally the most backward sector of the traditional societies, illiteracy is above 75 percent, and in a number of individual countries it rises to over 90. Illiteracy is also very high in much of Southwest Asia and Pakistan. Among the less developed countries, illiteracy drops below 50 percent in much of Latin America and in East Asia. It is between 50 and 75 percent in southern Africa and populous India.[1]

LANGUAGE AND RELIGION

Although religious affiliation and language prevalence are meaningful population characteristics, mapping them on a world scale presents serious problems.

Language is closely related to nationality and is a part of ethnicity. One's native language is not easily forgotten; it is one of the most enduring attributes of immigrants. Several thousand different languages are at present extant over the earth and many of these may be subdivided into still more numerous dialects. Any data on numbers of languages and numbers of people speaking them are bound to be only crude approximations.

It is far from easy to make sweeping generalizations relative to the significance of language as a population characteristic; there are too many exceptions to any simple and broadly applicable rules That a common language within a country fosters cohesion and strengthens nationalism is widely accepted. There can be no doubt either that language differences have in turn fostered separatism in some countries, among them Canada, Belgium, India, and Ceylon. Indeed, India is at present subdivided into a number of linguistic states. Yet Switzerland, with four languages, does not appear to have suffered in its development of national cohesion. Within strong nations there is a trend toward increased

[1] *World Population Data Sheet—1968*, Population Reference Bureau, Washington, D.C. See also *Compendium of Social Statistics*, United Nations, New York, 1963.

internal linguistic homogeneity. Moreover, the language of a militarily and commercially strong nation with a large colonial empire tends to become internationalized; English and French are prime examples.

Within the less developed realm linguistic diversity is especially characteristic of Negro Africa. To what degree this will be a handicap in that realm's development is hard to foresee. Asia, too, is an area of multiple languages, especially in the southeast and south where it has abetted separatist tendencies. Latin America, in contrast, has a high degree of linguistic homogeneity. Yet one can scarcely argue that this has operated to prevent political fracturing.

Where language and religion areally coincide, the two elements function to strengthen each other in their effects, and in combination the two forces doubly emphasize nationality. Doubtless, the approximate regional coincidence of the French language and Roman Catholicism in Canada tends to emphasize the separatist character of French Canada.

History furnishes many well-known instances of the religion of a population functioning as a motivating force. The spate of religious wars in medieval and early modern Europe, including the Cromwellian revolt in England, Christendom's Crusades against the "infidel" Moslems, and the close association of the Israelite people with the Hebrew faith are sufficient examples. Unquestionably the religious force was much stronger in earlier periods than it is today, although it still has significant strength. The partition of the subcontinent of India into the two states of Pakistan and India following World War II had as its basis the rivalries between Hindus and Moslems.

It seems fair to say that where religion has been concerned mainly with the well-being of mankind here on earth, and less with the saving of souls for a heavenly refuge after death, it has been a great force for good. But actually in numerous places and on numerous occasions the church departed from its humanitarian goal and strove instead for wealth and temporal power, engaged in ruinous factional jealousies and political intrigues, or was even guilty of taking human life in the name of religion. But, both for good and for bad, an indelible imprint of religion has been left upon human culture in various forms—holidays, folkways, customs, art, literature, architecture, food habits, politics, and the celebrations of weddings and funerals. The imprint is particularly strong where church and state were combined—in Spain and France, for example.

Religion has been a divisive as well as a unifying force. The Nazis were responsible for massacring nearly six million Jews. The hatred between Arab and Jew in the eastern Mediterranean lands is currently at the boiling point. Ireland is seriously split between the Catholic south and the Protestant north. And religion continues to play a role in such features as voting habits, the dissemination of birth control practices, and the degree of support for a separate parochial school system, even though its influence is shrinking.

In spite of the importance of religious affiliation as a population characteristic, religion is difficult to map and its world patterns hard to analyze. This is because, first, data on religions are very inadequate. In this respect it is noteworthy that a question on religious affiliation was dropped from the 1960 U.S. census because many people felt it was an intrusion upon their privacy. No such question has been included in the British census since 1851. In addition, what about religion should be mapped? Should it be the number of formal adherents, or only those who actively practice a particular faith? Or should the mapping be of those customs and habits that have religious origins? Few Scandinavians, for example, are active churchgoers, yet their culture has a strongly Protestant flavor. The same is true of Spain and France with their predominantly Roman Catholic heritage.

Four great religions dominate the earth's population:

Christianity	780,000,000 adherents
Buddhism	660,000,000 adherents
Hinduism	380,000,000 adherents
Islam	320,000,000 adherents

These are widely spread over the earth, to be sure, but the last three have fairly compact realms of dominance. Christianity prevails in the Western Hemisphere and in Europe, and there it has little competition, except widespread indifference to any formal religion. Buddhism is concentrated in East Asia, Hinduism in South Asia, and Islam in southwestern Asia, North Africa, and parts of southern and southeastern Asia. But the boundaries of these religious realms are indefinite, and homogeneous blocks are often lacking because of the important intermingling.

MOBILITY AND MIGRATION

That man is a mobile creature is evidenced by the racial, linguistic, and nationalistic mixing of so much of the earth's population. Mobility has always been a basic characteristic of population in all stages of its evolution, yet doubtless it has greatly increased with economic and technological progress, which in turn has expanded the efficiency of means of transport and communication. In turn, increased mobility has permitted increased migration. Still, for the great bulk of the earth's inhabitants a stationary type of life is the norm, even though great numbers do frequently change their place of residence, while many more engage in periodic and nonperiodic traveling. For a small minority of the earth's peoples, such as nomads and gypsies, a wandering existence is the rule.

Advanced societies are characterized by unusual mobility even though they are typically sedentary. In the United States, about one-quarter of the population does not live in the state where they were born, and every year one out of five persons changes his home.

Migration is not biologically determined and universal in the same sense that births and deaths are. All are born and all die, but only some migrate. Even when strong incentives to move are present, migration results only through an act of the human will. Moreover, those who move are not generally a cross section of the population left behind or entered. Migration is usually selective in terms of age, sex, and certain other characteristics, so that it results not merely in a shift in a certain number of persons representing a normal mix of population but usually also in a change in the social, occupational, and demographic structure of both the society invaded and that which was abandoned.

The term migration has various shades of meaning. Most commonly it is considered to involve a movement of some distance, which results in a change in permanent residence. But such a restrictive definition would operate to exclude other types of human mobility, including the daily trek of commuters between a city center and its peripheral areas, the seasonal shifts of migrant workers, the temporary and irregular movements of tourists, and the wanderings of pastoral nomads. Hence here the usual definition of migration is stretched so that it may include a wide range of population mobility, even though space may not permit a meaningful discussion of all forms.

Regrettably a discussion of human migration does not fit readily into a treatment of population which emphasizes world patterns of distribution. Migrations are specific and particular to individual continents, countries, regions, localities, and cities. Data needed for constructing a world map of current population mobility similar to maps of birth rates, rates of natural increase, or of literacy, are not available. Nor does information exist that will permit the comparison of population mobility in the various countries of the world. The recounting of numerous specific migrations, beginning with those dimly perceived outward movements of peoples from prehistoric diffusion centers down to the gargantuan population transfers involving scores of millions of people associated with World War II, would not serve our purpose, even though their consequences were enormous. Thus the brief account of human migration given here does not follow the usual geographic emphasis on distribution patterns. It is for this reason that the topic of migration is treated only briefly, and then mainly in terms of types, causes, consequences, and the like. The brevity of treatment is no indication that human migration is in any sense weak in its geographical importance. Indeed, it looms exceedingly large in any geographic analysis of the population element of a specific country or region.

Migratory Selection. In order to deal effectively with the causes, types, and consequences of migration it must first be pointed out why the migration process is a selective one. Assuming a sedentary population with an inducement to move, typically some individuals will leave and others remain where they are. But those who leave do not represent a random distribution of the biological and cultural characteristics of humanity in either the region of exit or entrance, for certain elements of the population tend to be more migratory than others. This is termed *migratory selection.*

Age of migrants is, without doubt, the most universally accepted migration differential. In both internal and international movements it is the young adults and late adolescents who ordinarily predominate. Of the millions of immigrants entering the United States during the nineteenth century, two-thirds to three-fourths were between 15 and 40 years of age. One reason for the predominance of young adults in most migrations is their greater adaptability to new conditions. And since they have only recently entered the labor force, they are also more amenable to a change of jobs. Because of age selectivity with emphasis on young adults, regions of in-migration are likely to have a disproportionately large number of young people. Regions of strong out-migration, on the other hand, from which the young have been drained away, probably will show a greater proportion of mature adults and oldsters. Thus Tokyo, a city of strong in-migration, has 37.6 percent of its population in the 15 to 29 age group, compared to 27.5 percent for Japan as a whole.

Migration is also likely to be sex selective, but whether those who move out are largely males or females depends on a variety of circumstances. There are no universally applicable rules. It is scarcely necessary to point out that where the out-migration is predominantly one of males, the region of departure becomes more strongly female, while the region of reception is characterized by an unduly large proportion of males. The reverse is true when females predominate among the out-migrants. In the nineteenth-century rural-urban migration in Europe, the movement was mainly one of young farm girls who found work as domestic servants in the cities. By contrast the frontier towns of the American

West a century ago attracted mainly young males. For example, in Colorado in 1860, only slightly more than 3 percent of the population were women in the reproductive ages. But while it is easy to cite specific cases of male or female selectivity among migrants, one must be wary of generalizations. There is some validity no doubt in the generalization that in less developed countries migrants are predominantly male, whether the movement be international or intranational. All the large commercial and industrial cities of India show a strong male predominance. The same is true in the newer settlements and mining towns of Negro Africa where males may outnumber females two or three to one. In the economically more advanced countries, on the other hand, short-distance internal migrants are likely to be predominantly female, whereas long-distance internal migrants are mainly male. Males are also more numerous among international migrants. Cities specializing in heavy industry are likely to attract an undue proportion of males. But other cities specializing in the tertiary or service industries, of which Washington, D.C., is a prime example, are more attractive to females.

Migratory selection operates also in terms of marital status. The usual generalization is that migrants are weighted on the side of *single* young adults. This was probably more true of the Western world in earlier periods than it is today. Then female domestic servants and male pioneers were mostly unmarried transients who stood in contrast to the relatively fixed families. In the less developed parts of the world the migrants are still predominantly young, unmarried males. But in the economically advanced regions the married seem to be about as mobile as the single persons and often the motivation for the move is related to the family life, as the search is made for better schools and houses, more desirable neighborhoods, and employment providing higher status or greater income.

Further, some occupation groups seem more likely to migrate than do others, although here broad generalizations are not numerous. Where migration is economically motivated it is to be expected that selectivity on the basis of employment will be stronger than when the motivation lies elsewhere. Skilled and semiskilled workers are inclined to be more migratory than are the unskilled. Professional people are among the more mobile classes, whereas officials, proprietors, and managers are distinctly less so. It is less of a wrench for the foot-loose unemployed to move than for those who are anchored by a job.

Migratory selection possibly operates also with respect to intelligence, mental health, educational attainment, nationality, and race, and very likely other characteristics as well. But generalizations about selective effects are usually valid only for specific migrations. Ordinarily, selection seems to depend more upon conditions at the place of destination than upon those at the place of departure.[2]

Migration and Population Growth. The effect of migration on population growth in the regions of origin and of destination are exceedingly complex. If 1000 persons move from region *A* to region *B*, it might on first thought appear that the only effect will be for the population of *B* to increase by 1000 and that of *A* to decrease by the same amount. But because, as has been shown, migrations operate selectively, the assumed shift of 1000 persons from *A* to *B* will probably carry in its train changes in the age and sex structures of the population and the social conditions and economies of both the exit and entrance regions, which will in turn influence the future populations of each. These indirect effects cause the relation between migrations and population growth to be highly complex. It is because migrants are characteristically youths or young adults that their departure typically means a rise in the average age in the region of exit and so an increase in the death rate and a fall in the birth rate. The opposite is true of the region of reception. As a consequence the shift of 1000 inhabitants will usually mean a total change of the populations by far more than the figure seems to indicate.

The effects of migration on population growth in the region of exodus depends on circumstances. To the degree that emigration causes a relief from population pressure it can alter the determinants of growth. Out-migration from populous and densely populated countries like China or India can have almost no effect on the numbers remaining, for those departing will shortly be replaced through a small reduction in infant mortality resulting from a slight improvement in economic conditions. But in nineteenth-century western Europe, where population pressure was weaker and mortality was under much better control, it is open to question whether the mass migration overseas of tens of millions resulted in a significant depression in death rates. But by making earlier marriage possible for many couples it may have elevated the fertility rate somewhat. If emigration eases population pressure to bring about change in either fertility or mortality, the change in population growth in the region of exodus will be nullified to some degree.[3] But if the death rate was already low and the small-family system well established, then the resulting decrease in numbers from emigration can be great because of the loss of potential young parents.

The effects of migration on population growth in the region of in-migration are also circumstantial. The shift of some 50 to 60 million

---

[2] William Petersen, *Population*, Macmillan, New York, 1961, p. 603.

[3] Petersen, *Population*, p. 603.

TABLE 5.1   Proportion of Total Increase
in Population of the United States Due
to Net Migration

Decade	Net Migration (percent)
1870–1880	25.4
1880–1890	38.8
1890–1900	28.4
1900–1910	39.4
1910–1920	18.1
1920–1930	18.7
1930–1940	−0.95
1940–1950	7.2

SOURCE: Taeuber and Taeuber, "Changing Population," Table 91, p.
294.

people from Europe chiefly to the Western Hemisphere during the
nineteenth and twentieth centuries would appear to greatly swell growth
in the new lands overseas. The United States is a prime example of a
country an important part of whose added population over the eight
decades from 1870 to 1950 resulted from in-migration. In two decades
the proportion of the total increase resulting from in-migration was
nearly 40 percent (Table 5.1). But by how much immigration eventually
increased the population of the United States is a topic that has been
actively debated. Some have even argued that the competition of immigrant laborers resulted in a decline in the native birth rate, so that if the
foreigners had not come the native element would have filled the places
which the foreigners took over. It seems likely, however, that the influx
from overseas to this sparsely settled country generally increased the
population, although not necessarily by the same amount as the number
of foreigners entering. It might have been even larger, however, because
of the newcomers' youngish age structure and their tendency to have
larger families.

To recapitulate, there are three aspects of the relationship between
migration and population growth: (1) the movement of the migrants
themselves; (2) the effects of the migration upon age structure; and (3)
its effects on socioeconomic conditions in the regions of exodus and
reception, which in turn may modify the results of the transfer.[4]

[4] Petersen, *Population*, p. 606.

Types of Migration. Any classification of migrations by cause is difficult to formulate since the stimulating factors are so numerous, varied, and overlapping. Bogue [5] enumerates 25 migration-stimulating situations, 15 factors in choosing a destination, and 10 socioeconomic conditions that may affect mobility. Still his list is far from complete. However, even an exhaustive list could not aid in weighing the relative importance of the several factors influencing the decision of the migrant. A rough first step in developing a typology of migration in which movement-stimulating factors are related to probable effects is to differentiate between "push" and "pull" factors, that is, between the conditions at the region of origin that repel and those at the destination that attract. The relevance of this distinction is of importance only for sedentary peoples; for nomads it is much less so. The concept of "push" and "pull" factors is also inadequate because such factors usually comprise a miscellaneous array of items; these are often so unrelated they defy distinction and many times fail to differentiate even between personal motives and social causes. The push-pull dichotomy can form the basis for a satisfactory typology of migration only when it has been refined to distinguish between people who move in order to gain the new (*innovating* migration), and on the other hand, those who leave in order to retain what they have at home (*conservative* migration). The migrant's level of aspiration should also be included in the analysis. Five general classes of migration are recognized, designated by Petersen [6] as primitive, forced, impelled, free, and mass. The precise meaning given to these terms needs some elaboration.

Primitive migration refers to a movement resulting from an ecological push; it is related to man's inability to cope with the natural conditions of his environment. Usually primitive migration is associated with prehistoric or preindustrial peoples having primitive cultures. Such migrations were often *conservative*, as the term has been defined, for there was a strong tendency for the migrating group to search out an environment similar to the one it was abandoning: pastoral peoples usually chose to stay with grasslands; agrarian populations looked for other similar agricultural locations. The treks of prehistoric primitives may be designated as *wandering*. Movements of contemporary primitives are called *gathering* if the people are food gatherers and hunters, or *nomadism* if

[5] D. J. Bogue, Internal Migration, in P. M. Hauser and O. D. Duncan (eds.), *The Study of Population: an Inventory and Appraisal,* University of Chicago Press, Chicago, 1959.

[6] Petersen, *Population,* pp. 609–621. See also William Petersen, "A General Typology of Migration," *Am. Soc. Rev.,* Vol. 23, June 1958, pp. 256–266. The remainder of this discussion on migration is based mainly on Petersen's arguments.

TABLE 5.2   General Typology of Migration

Type of Interaction	Migratory Force	Class of Migration	Type of Migration	
			Conservative	Innovating
Nature and man	Ecological push	Primitive	Wandering Gatherers and Nomads	Flight from the land
State (or equivalent) and man	Migration policy	Impelled Forced	Flight Displacement	Coolie trade Slave trade
Man and his norms	Higher aspirations	Free	Group	Pioneer
Collective behavior	Social momentum	Mass	Settlement	Urbanization

SOURCE: Petersen, *Population* (2nd rev. ed.), Macmillan, 1969. Table 8–9, p. 298.

they move with their flocks and herds. In the modern era the destination of many migrating agriculturists has often been a town or city, and hence that movement is classed as *innovating* rather than conservative, and represents a *flight from the land* (see Table 5.2).

Many times the agent stimulating movement is the state or a social institution. Here our typology recognizes two classes: *forced migration*, when the migrants have no choice in whether they go or stay, and *impelled migration*, when they retain some power of decision. If the function of the movement, as defined by the activating agent, is simply to get rid of the people, it resembles conservative migration. Its two subtypes are *flight* (e.g., before invading armies), or *displacement*, which involves the forcible removal of a hostile population. Such movement was resorted to on a grand scale by the Nazis. But if the people are moved in order to use their labor elsewhere, and so involves a shift in behavior patterns, the migration is classed as innovating. This may be either of the *slave trade* type if forced, or the *coolie trade* type if impelled (see Tables 5.2 and 5.3).

Free migration finds its activating agent in the will of the migrants and not in some outside force. Free migration usually involves rather small numbers, for individuals strongly motivated by the zest for adventure or for personal improvement are not abundant. Two subdivisions are *pioneer migration*, usually innovating in character, and *group*

TABLE 5.3   Migratory Selection by Type of Migration

Types	Destination of Migrants	Migratory Selection	Comments; Examples
Wandering			
Wandering of peoples	None	Survival of the fittest?	Prehistoric migrations
Marine wandering	None	Same	Same
Ranging			
Gathering	Greener pastures; commutation	None	Migratory way of life
Nomadism		None	Same
Flight from the land	More fertile land (or towns)	?	Malthusian pressure
Flight	Place of safety	None; or minority groups	Emigrés and refugees
Coolie trade	Site of work, usually plantations	Young males	Large remigration
Displacement	Any	None; or minority groups	Population exchanges
Slave trade	Site of work	Young adults	Mercantile or industrial
Pioneers	Frontier lands	Young males	Individually motivated
Group migration	New lands	Dissident groups	Same
Settlement	Rural areas	Young males predominate	Social momentum
Urbanization	Towns	Young females predominate (in the West)	Same

SOURCE: Petersen, *Population* (2nd rev. ed.), Macmillan, 1969, Table 8–10, p. 300.

migration, which is more often conservative. Pioneer migration from Europe to the New World in the nineteenth century, involving risks that were both great and unable to be foreseen, tended to attract mainly romantics, adventurers, or intellectuals impelled by their ideals. It was these pioneer migrants who blazed the trail and set the stage for the more voluminous mass migrations to follow. This first stage gradually developed into the second one of group migration. Sometimes these groups were church congregations in the homeland, but more commonly they represented emigrants who drew together for mutual aid and protection as they faced the hazards of the New World frontier.

Mass migration as a class is illustrated by the greatly swollen stream of migrants from Europe to America which followed upon the heels of the earlier and smaller pioneer and group migrations. Mass migration, representing as it did a social pattern and collective behavior, involved little in the way of individual motivation. It became so much the established pattern that it came to be known as "America fever." There are two types of mass migration, classified according to the nature of the destination of the migrants: a conservative *settlement* type involving those who became farmers or village merchants or artisans, and an innovating *urbanization* type, which included those going to the larger cities. The rural-urban movement so typical of the modern era is much the same, whether it involves an intranational or an international transfer.

Nonpermanent Population Movements. When there is a need to distinguish between the "permanent" *migrant* and the temporary *traveler,* this is sometimes done by arbitrarily defining the migrant as one who removes for a year or more. Although this definition is based only on convenience, it does allow for those short-duration population movements, usually rhythmic in character and motivated by work or pleasure, which do not fit the more standard concept of migration as an uprooting process. Some of these were mentioned earlier.

One cyclical type of travel is annual in its periodicity and is tied to the march of the seasons. Some *seminomadism,* where the tribe and its flocks or herds follow the advance and retreat of the rain season in search of animal forage is of this type. *Transhumance* is another form of seasonal population movement associated with the pastoral industry. It involves a temporary transfer of people, together with their flocks and herds, from their permanent farmsteads in the lowlands to the mountain pastures in summer after the snow has melted. They move downward to the cultivated and more protected valleys again as winter approaches. In some regions of cultivated crops peak seasonal demands for agricultural labor, usually for harvesting, induce large-scale seasonal movements of workers and their families. In the United States, some

1,000,000 migrants (including their families) make the annual pilgrimage northward across state lines as the harvests of various crops peak. They have their origin in the states along the southern border. It is essentially a young labor force (half the migrants are under 25 years of age); more than 70 percent are male; and 80 percent are white. The return southward trek occurs in fall as the harvests come to an end. With the increased mechanization of agriculture, the use of such migrant labor appears to be on the decline.

Diurnal movements of workers, by contrast, are on the increase, both in numbers involved and in distance traveled. The daily flow of urban workers from their places of residence toward their places of work, mainly in the central business district, in the early morning, and the return ebb of this same group in late afternoon, are characteristic features of the city and its peripheral regions. This is known as *commuting*. Efficient transportation has made this huge commuter population transfer possible, while the rapid urbanization of much of the world has made it increasingly necessary. Around London commuting range extends outward from the city's core for 70 miles or more.

In addition to the periodic annual and diurnal movements of people there are those swelling hordes of humanity whose nonperiodic travels are associated mainly with vacations, fun, or business. Earlier, the trek to new environments—in mountains, along sea coasts, by lakes and streams, or even abroad—as people sought pleasure and relaxation was mainly a summer affair. Now it is becoming more widely spread over the entire year. Formerly it involved chiefly the affluent; in recent decades it has come to include also the less prosperous, whose numbers are far greater.

RESIDENCE: RURAL-URBAN

Residence refers to the nature of the settlement in which a person dwells. It is not in itself a characteristic of population, but it is as a result of one's residence that a person develops certain personality traits, points of view, and ways of thinking which, when applied to large groups of people, are then recognized as population characteristics. An individual's residence in a rural as compared with an urban environment unquestionably develops in him some of his most distinguishing characteristics. Rural society presents sharp contrasts to that of urban places in such features as size of settlement clusters, population density, degree of ethnic and cultural homogeneity, and occupational and social stability. The ways of life of the two groups are different. The rural dweller is more exposed to the impact of nature, both its good and bad features;

the urbanite has greater protection. The farmer has fewer social contacts with others, and those he does have are likely to be more local, and with people in his own stratum. Admittedly "urban" and "rural" as ideal types of society are in the nature of mental constructs which deviate from reality. No actual society is either wholly rural or completely urban. Town and country today are not entirely in opposition to each other in residence, occupation, and way of life. But as an ideal type, urban continues to represent a state of mind, a group of traditions and customs, and the many attitudes that are inseparable from these customs. Any universal causes and effects of urbanism and ruralism are hard to establish, for they differ between countries and peoples.

It should be made clear that the study of cities as entities—their numbers, size classes, spacing, distribution, and internal and functional structure areas—belongs to the field of settlement geography. Here it is urban population en masse that is being considered, not its individual agglomerations.

Definition and Classification. Society cannot be readily divided into clearly identifiable rural and urban groups—the line of demarcation is far from sharp. Instead, society resembles a spectrum or continuum in which clearly rural attributes are polarized at one extreme and those distinctly urban at the other, the proportions of each changing only very gradually between the two. By the various criteria used to distinguish rural from urban, society becomes gradually less rural and more urban as one passes from the isolated farmstead through stages represented by hamlet, village, market town, city, and finally metropolis. Then of course there is that very numerous group in the industrialized countries, the rural nonfarm people, whose residence is in the country but whose work is in the town or city, a situation that requires daily commuting.

Thus it is no wonder that the definitions of rural and urban vary greatly among countries, making international comparisons difficult. In some countries the rural-urban definition is based on the type of local government; others relate it to the total population within minor administrative subdivisions; still others base it upon size of a population cluster expressed in numbers of people. But this scarcely ends the confusion, for there remains the bewildering array of specific national definitions within the three general types noted. Size of settlement is the most respected type of definition for rural-urban, and this is the one adopted by the United Nations in its publications.

Yet this does not solve the question of a line of demarcation between a rural and an urban population cluster. For most countries the dividing line is probably a settlement population somewhere between 1000 and 5000—the United States and Mexico use 2500, Japan and India about

5000, Argentina, 2000, Canada, 1000, and Denmark, 250. However, data for such small settlements are not available for many countries, so for international comparisons the United Nations has defined *urban population* as the population living in localities of 20,000 or more inhabitants. But while such data are available as of about 1960 for nearly all countries in the more developed regions, they are lacking for more than half of the population of the less developed realm, or a little less than 40 percent of the earth's people.[7] For this reason many authors, for international comparisons, define urban as that part of the population dwelling in cities of 100,000 or more inhabitants. But it must be clear that neither 20,000 or 100,000 can be a universally accurate demarcation separating rural from urban. For the earth as a whole these figures are set too high, and hence tend to underreport the urban component, especially in the economically more advanced countries. Moreover, when urban-population counts are made on the basis of the political city, generally urban population is underestimated and rural population exaggerated, for urbanites living beyond the city limits are becoming very numerous.

The Urbanization Process. *The level of urbanization* is defined as the *proportion* of total population residing in urban places (i.e., those of 20,000 or more inhabitants, or in communities otherwise defined). It does not refer to absolute urban numbers. The *urbanization process* denotes an increase in the fraction of a population which is urban. The *rate of urbanization* is the percent increase over a given period in the proportion of total population living in urban communities. Cities and their populations can grow without any advance in urbanism if the rural population grows at an equal or greater rate.

Trends in World Urbanization. The recency and speed of world urbanization is a striking feature of the modern era. The earliest cities had their beginnings about 5500 years ago, so the urban process is not new. But over nearly the whole period of human history since then the process of urbanization has inched forward only very slowly. Before the Industrial Revolution, because agricultural surpluses were small and urban people had little to exchange with the rural folk, towns were few. With technical progress, industrialization became possible, and this together with enlarged agricultural surpluses led to a marked acceleration in urbanization. As late as 1800 it is estimated that only about 3 percent of the earth's population lived in towns of over 5000 population, and 2.4

[7] *World Survey of Rural and Urban Population*, United Nations Doc. E/CN./187, March 8, 1965, pp. 6–8; 20. Slightly different data on urban population are provided in *Urban and Rural Population Growth, 1920–1960, with Projections*, United Nations Population Division, Working Paper No. 15, September, 1967.

TABLE 5.4 Total World Population and World Urban Population: 1800–1980

Year	Total World Population (millions)	Population Living in Localities of 20,000 Inhabitants or More		Population Living in Localities of 20,000 to 100,000 Inhabitants		Population Living in Localities of 100,000 Inhabitants or more	
		Millions	Percent of World Population	Millions	Percent of World Population	Millions	Percent of World Population
1800	906	21.7	2.4	6.1	0.7	15.6	1.7
1850	1,171	50.4	4.3	22.9	2.0	27.5	2.3
1900	1,608	147.9	9.2	59.3	3.7	88.6	5.5
1950	2,400	502.2	20.9	188.5	7.8	313.7	13.1
1960	2,998	753.0	25.1	—	—	—	—
1980	4,330	1,380.0	31.9	—	—	—	—

SOURCES: U.N., *World Social Situation*, 1957, p. 114.
U.N., *World Social Situation*, 1967 (advance copy), p. 35

TABLE 5.5 Percent of Increase in Total World Population and in World Urban Population: 1800–1850, 1850–1900, 1900–1950

Years	Total World Population Percent Increase	World Population Living in Agglomerations of 20,000 Inhabitants or More Percent Increase	World Population Living in Agglomerations of 100,000 Inhabitants or More Percent Increase
1800–1850	29.2	132.3	76.3
1850–1900	37.3	193.5	222.2
1900–1950	49.3	239.6	254.1

SOURCE: U.N., *World Social Situation*, 1957, p. 114.

percent in cities of 20,000 and over. The second figure (2.4) slightly less than doubled from 1800 to 1850 (4.3 percent); more than doubled between 1850 and 1900 (9.2 percent), more than doubled again (20.9 percent) in the first half of the twentieth century, and the rate of change from 1950 to 1960 was twice that of the preceding 50 years.[8] In 1960 the proportion of the earth's population living in urban places of all sizes is estimated to have been about 33 percent. By 1990 it is estimated the fraction of the world's people living in large places of over 100,000 will be more than half. Of course, the proportion will be significantly larger if the definition of urban is lowered to 20,000 or 5000. So the rate of world urban growth has been ever accelerating since 1800 and it probably will continue to accelerate for some time to come. It is significant that the period of acceleration was contemporaneous with the Industrial-Scientific Revolution.

Origin of the Increased Numbers of Urbanites. In the urbanization process covering the last century and a half or more, it is fair to ask where the swelling flood of urbanites came from. There appear to be three possibilities accounting for the rise in the proportion of total population living in cities:

1. Many rural settlements grow so large they are reclassified as towns and cities.
2. The excess of births over deaths is greater in urban than in rural places.
3. People move from the country to the city.

The effect of the first was slight; the second never existed; so the only large source for city growth was net migration.[9] Why did the swarming

[8] Kingsley Davis, "The Urbanization of the Human Population," *Scientific American*, Vol. 213, July 1965, p. 11.
[9] Davis, "Urbanization," p. 44.

to the cities, involving a huge rural-urban migration of population, assume such large proportions during the modern period, contemporaneous with the Industrial Revolution? Every country affected by the Industrial Revolution experienced this same large flow of people from farm to cities, caused by several forces combining and interacting. Fundamental is the fact that human productivity was greatly expanded by technological improvement, and this, in conjunction with certain constant factors, favored urban concentration. One of the constant factors is that agriculture, which uses land as its main instrument of production, tends to diffuse population. By contrast, urban activities—manufacturing, construction, commerce, services—use land only as a site of operation, and gain advantage by locating close together in cities. Moreover, the market for agricultural products is less expansible than the demand for manufactures and services. Thus as productivity grew, the manpower requirements of agriculture waned, but much more labor could be absorbed by manufacturing, construction, commerce, and services that attract by their relatively higher wages. This in turn served to entice disadvantaged manpower from the rural areas. Due to a prolonged decline in mortality the rural areas became full to overflowing, and this excess population was attracted to the burgeoning cities where economic opportunities were brighter. But the push from the burdened farming districts was sometimes sufficient to cause migration even when employment was not promptly available in the cities. Such is the situation today in many less developed countries.

The Cycle of Urbanization. Urbanization is a cyclical process through which nations pass as they evolve from agrarian to industrial societies. The urbanization process, involving as it does an increase in the *proportion* of urbanites, has a beginning and an end. The growth of cities and the absolute numbers of their urban people, however, have no apparent limit. In most of the advanced nations, intensive urbanization began within the last 100 years or a little more. Rate of urban growth attained its highest point in England and in the Low Countries during the first half of the nineteenth century. An accelerated rate is typical of the less developed regions only in the twentieth century. In some advanced countries the end of the urbanization cycle is now in sight, for while the number of urban people is still growing, their proportion in the whole population is near static, or even declining. Thus the typical urbanization curve resembles a weak S ($\int$). Normally as the proportion of urban people climbs above 50 percent the curve loses steepness, and after 75 percent it flattens or even declines.[10] The rate of urbaniza-

---

[10] Davis, "Urbanization," p. 44.

tion began to slacken in England after 1861, in Belgium after 1910, and in Sweden after 1920.

Toward the end of the cycle there is some ambiguity in the urbanization process resulting from so many urbanites having residences in the country. In some degree, therefore, the slowing down of urbanization may be more apparent than real. As excellent commutation systems permit an increasing number who work in the city to live in the country, rural society contains an ever larger proportion of urbanites. Rural non-farm population comes to increase as fast as the city population, and so the urbanization curve flattens. In addition, the farm population is no longer sufficient to furnish migrants for the cities. But, as indicated earlier, cessation of urbanization does not necessarily mean a halting of city growth; it merely indicates that urban population is growing only about as fast as the general population, or perhaps even slower.

Urbanization in the Less Developed and the More Developed Realms. As of about 1960 some 700 million persons, or about one-quarter of the world's population, lived in urban places (defined as communities of 20,000 or more inhabitants).[11] This is an increase of about 39 percent above the estimated urban population of 500 million in 1950. The economically more developed regions of the world were more than twice as urbanized, on the average, in 1960 as the less developed regions of Asia, Africa, and Latin America (Table 5.6). Of the three less developed continents, Africa was the least urbanized and Latin America the most. But there were wide differences in degrees of urbanization among the countries in each continent.

During the 1950s urban population grew most rapidly in the less developed regions. In them, as a group, urban population increased at an average rate of about 5.5 percent annually, as against only about 2.5 percent in the economically more advanced regions, even though in many of the latter the definition of an urban place was broadened to include the residents in suburban and fringe areas. Rural population was also growing more rapidly in the less developed realm than in the more developed one, but in spite of this the less developed peoples were urbanizing more rapidly, that is, the proportionate share of urban population in the total was increasing at a faster rate in the traditional societies than in the economically more advanced ones. But although the rate of urbanization was more rapid in the three less developed continents during the 1950s than in earlier decades, acceleration of the trend was not true in all countries of these continents. However, data are not adequate for

[11] U.N., *World Survey*, 1965, p. 3. See also, U.N., *Urban and Rural Population Growth*, 1967.

TABLE 5.6 The Degree of Urbanization in the World, 1950 and 1960 (places with 20,000 or more inhabitants)

Regions	Level of Urbanization [a] (percent of total population)		Percent of Increase [b]	Net Rural-Urban Migration, 1950–1960 as a Percentage [c] of:		Percent Increase in Total Population [d]	Percent Increase in Urban Population
	1950	1960		1950 Rural Population	1950 Urban Population		
World total	21	25	17	5	20	19	39
More developed regions	37	41	10	7	11	14	25
North America	43	46	6	5	7	20	27
Europe (excluding U.S.S.R.)	37	40	8	5	9	8	17
Northwestern	52	54	3	4	3	8	11
Central	37	40	9	6	10	10	20
Southern	23	27	16	5	17	8	25
U.S.S.R.	31	36	17	9	20	19	39
Oceania	46	53	15	16	19	24	43
Australia and New Zealand	58	65	12	21	15	25	40
Remainder of Oceania		3					11
Less developed regions	14	18	28	6	34	21	55
Africa	10	13	37	5	46	23	69
North	21	26	23	8	29	25	54
South, West, and East	6	9	50	4	61	22	3
Asia	14	18	26	5	31	20	51
Excluding China (Mainland)	17	19 [e]	15	4	18	22	40
China (Mainland)	10	15	50	6	57	15	72
Latin America	25	32	28	12	36	30	66
Argentina, Chile, Uruguay	47	56	19	21	23	22	45
Remainder of Latin America	21	28	33	12	41	31	72

SOURCES: U.N., *World Survey*, Table 3; Bourgeois-Pichat, *Growth and Development*, pp. 35, 40.

[a] Range of estimated values results from alternative estimates for Mainland China.
[b] Percentage increase computed from unrounded data.
[c] The data in these columns did not appear in the preliminary United Nations report, but are based on Bourgeois-Pichat's own calculations.
[d] Calculated on the basis of data contained in the *U.N. Demographic Yearbook*, 1964, Table 2.
[e] Computed from unrounded data.

determining to what extent the trend of rising rates of urbanization prevailed.

Although at present the more developed regions have less than one-third of the world's people, they had over half of the urban population during the first half of the twentieth century. But by 1960, more than half of the city people were in the less developed regions. In many countries in Latin America and Africa, and to a somewhat lesser extent in Asia, the urban population is concentrated to an unusual degree in a single primate city; it is more widely spread among cities of different size classes in the economically more developed nations. Not only is the ratio of urban to total population increasing more rapidly in the less developed countries than in the industrial nations, but it is even more rapid than was the nineteenth-century surge of urbanization in industrial nations, although the differential is not large.

In terms of *absolute* growth of urban population, cities in the backward countries are growing more than twice as fast (about 4.5 percent annually, 1940 to 1960) as did western Europe during its period of most rapid urban population growth (about 2.1 percent).[12] Further, the absolute growth rate of city population in the traditional societies is currently more than twice as rapid as the proportional growth of urban population to the total population. This reflects the fact that the total population growth of the less developed countries is twice as great as that of the advanced nations. Thus nearly half of the urban population increase in less developed nations is due to general population growth (rural plus urban) alone, and the remainder to migration (Table 5.6).

At an earlier period, in the European countries, only about 20± percent was due to general growth, and around 70± percent to rural-urban migration.[13] Cities in the Western industrial countries required a huge influx of people from rural areas if they were to grow. But rural-urban migration plays a less important role in the current accelerating urbanization of the poorer countries. And yet, if the explosive growth of overall population in the backward countries is not to pile up economically absurd densities on rural land, there must of necessity be a high rate of migration to the cities. It seems unlikely that any of the backward nations in the future will need more than 25 or 30 percent of its population in primary production, if that much; yet at present many of them have 50 to 75 percent so employed. The dilemma is clear. If a huge exodus from the land is not forthcoming, the rural areas will be swamped. But if a mighty rural-urban migration is generated to save the country-

[12] U.N., *World Survey*, 1965, p. 49.
[13] U.N., *World Survey*, 1965, p. 50.

side, then the cities will be submerged. In the advanced countries the earlier rapid urbanization was painful to be sure, but it did act to solve the problem of a swelling rural population. This is not true in the poor countries today. Obviously, the only solution is a drastic reduction in human multiplication. In contrast to the European situation of a century or more earlier, no important relief can be expected from out-migration, for no large and desirable empty spaces remain on the earth, with the possible exception of parts of the humid tropics.

Thus both urbanization and absolute urban growth are proceeding rapidly in the less developed world. But does this urbanization resemble that which occurred earlier in Europe? Is it closely related to cultural and economic change as was true in the Western world? It would seem not, for the rate of urbanization shows no consistent relationship with such economic indexes as growth of manufacturing, capital accumulation, or increases in agricultural productivity. Actually urbanization rates in cities of over 100,000 within the less developed realm vary directly with the proportions of the economically active population employed in primary production, and is inversely related to per capita income, to the average per capita caloric intake, and to the percent of manufactures within total domestic output.[14] Such relationships suggest that rapid urbanization and rapid growth of cities had begun in the less developed regions before there was any significant upturn in economic growth.

What, then, if not economic expansion, is providing the stimulation for accelerated urbanization in the poorer countries? One factor is the great expansion of governmental functions and the supplanting of foreign by native personnel in the burgeoning bureaucracies. Another is the plummeting of the death rate with the spread of Western sanitation and medicine. This in turn has created a large excess of people in the countryside; some then drift to the cities in search of employment. But as yet the cities are not in need of a greatly expanded labor force, with the result that the great mass of migrants eke out a miserable existence on the shanty-town fringes of the larger cities.

Distribution of Urbanism and of Urban Population. From the preceding discussion is evident that world distribution patterns of urban population may be expressed in more than one way. One may choose to show the absolute magnitude of the urban population living on the earth's continents, countries, or other designated regions. Or one might prefer to represent the urban population element in the form of a ratio of urban numbers to total inhabitants. The latter is an expression of the intensity of urbanization and of course omits any suggestion of the

[14] Amos H. Hawley, World Urbanization: Trends and Prospects, in Ronald Freedman (ed.), *Population: The Vital Revolution*, Aldine, Chicago, 1965, p. 78.

TABLE 5.7 Population in Large Cities (100,000 and Over) by Major Continental Regions

Area	1800 In Millions	1800 As Percent of Total Population	1850 In Millions	1850 As Percent of Total Population	1900 In Millions	1900 As Percent of Total Population	1950 In Millions	1950 As Percent of Total Population	1960 In Millions	1960 As Percent of Total Population
World	15.6	1.7	27.5	2.3	88.6	5.5	313.7	13.1	601.5	20.1
Asia	9.8	1.6	12.2	1.7	19.4	2.1	105.6	7.5	207.4	12.6
Europe a	5.4	2.9	13.2	4.9	48.0	11.9	118.2	19.9	186.0	29.1
Africa	0.30	0.3	0.25	0.2	1.4	1.1	10.2	5.2	30.1	11.0
America	0.13	0.4	1.8	3.0	18.6	12.8	74.6	22.6	170.3	41.4
Oceania	—	—	—	—	1.3	21.7	5.1	39.2	7.7	49.0

SOURCES: U.N., *World Social Situation*, 1957, p. 114; *U.N. Demographic Yearbook*, 1966.
a Including U.S.S.R.

absolute size of the urban population of a country or region. The first method is crude, for comparing absolute urban values for regions of vastly different sizes and total populations leaves much to be desired.

In any distribution analysis of urban population many of the data used are, of necessity, estimates. Based upon places of 20,000 or more inhabitants in 1960, it is believed that slightly over half (51–53 percent) of the world's urban people were in the three underdeveloped continents (Table 5.9). Populous Asia alone may have contained 36–39 percent. On first thought this may seem odd, considering the weak intensity of urbanization there. But the low ratio of urbanites is offset by the prodigious total population, amounting to about 56 percent of the earth's humanity. Ranking next to Asia in numbers of city dwellers is industrialized Europe, with 23–24 percent (34–35 percent if U.S.S.R. is in-

TABLE 5.8 Distribution of the World Urban Population by Large Geographic Regions, 1950, 1960

	Distribution of the Total World Population (percent)		Distribution of the World Urban Population			
			Population Living in Localities of 20,000 Inhabitants and More (percent)		Population Living in Localities of 100,000 Inhabitants and More (percent)	
	1950	1960	1950	1960	1950	1960
Asia	53.2	55.3	33.8	34.4	33.7	34.4
Europe [a]	16.4	14.2	27.5	25.6	26.5	20.4
Anglo-America	6.8	6.6	13.9	15.8	15.2	18.8
U.S.S.R.	8.1	7.1	12.0	10.9	11.2	10.6
South America	4.6	5.5	5.8	6.9	6.5	7.1
Africa	8.2	9.2	3.7	3.7	3.2	5.0
Middle America	2.1	1.6	2.1	2.6	2.0	2.4
Oceania	0.5	0.5	1.2	1.1	1.6	1.3

SOURCES: U.N., *World Social Situation*, 1957, p. 115; *U.N. Demographic Yearbook*, 1966; Urban and Rural Population Growth, 1920–1966, with Projections, U.N. Population Division, Working Paper No. 15, September, 1967, pp. 17 and 128.

[a] Except the U.S.S.R.

TABLE 5.9   Estimated Percent Distribution of World Total and Urban
Population by Regions, 1950 and 1960

| | Distribution of World Total Population (percent) | | Distribution of Population in Places of 20,000 and More Inhabitants (percent) | | |
| | | | | 1960 | |
	1950	1960	1950	China (Mainland) Estimated to be 10 Percent Urban	China (Mainland) Estimated to be 15 Percent Urban
Less developed regions	70	72	48	51	53
Africa	9	9	4	5	5
Asia	55	56	36	36	39
Excluding China (Mainland)	33	34	26	27	26
China (Mainland)	22	22	10	9	13
Latin America	6	7	8	10	9
More developed regions	30	28	52	49	47
Northern America	7	7	13	13	12
Europe (excluding U.S.S.R.)	16	14	27	24	23
U.S.S.R.	7	7	11	11	11
Oceania	—[a]	—[a]	1	1	1

SOURCE: U.N., World Survey, 1965.
[a] Less than 1 percent.

cluded), followed by Anglo-America with 12–13 percent, U.S.S.R. (11
percent), Latin America (9–10), Africa (5), and Oceania (1).

Employing countries rather than continents, and cities of 100,000+
instead of 20,000+, the United States heads the list with 17–18 percent
of the world's urban people (Table 5.10). Then follows U.S.S.R. with
10–11 percent, Mainland China (nearly 10), Japan and India (7–8), and
the United Kingdom (4–5). In some instances the relatively high rank
in number of dwellers in large cities reflects mainly the intensity of
urbanization, as in the United States and Britain. In other instances, it relates to the magnitude of total population. In still others, it is a combination of the two.

We turn now from a measurement of urban in terms of numbers of

TABLE 5.10   Total Population Living in Localities
100,000 Inhabitants and More (About 1960–1965)

	Million	Percent of World Urban
United States	104.2	17.3
U.S.S.R.	63.6	10.6
Mainland China	59.4	9.9
Japan	46.2	7.7
India	42.4	7.1
United Kingdom	27.2	4.5

SOURCE: *U.N. Demographic Yearbook, 1965.*

city dwellers to one that involves the intensity of urbanization (ratio of urban people to total population) based upon places of 20,000 or more inhabitants. In our typology of world urbanism, four levels are recognized—low, medium low, medium high, and high. The chosen separation points are 20, 30, and 40 percent urban. The urbanization values of the world's countries range from lows of 5 percent and under to highs in excess of 60 percent. Within this range of national values there is a relatively strong clustering of the less developed countries at the low end of the scale and of the more developed ones at the high end. Still the polarization is by no means complete. Of the three less developed continents, urbanization is at the lowest level in Africa and highest in Latin America. Recent data on urbanization, based on cities of 20,000 or more population, are lacking for two to three score of the less developed countries. This fact is revealed by the numerous blank spaces in Fig. 5.2 on page 162.

Type 1 (low urbanization; under 20 percent) includes 43 of the 72 less developed countries comprising the typology.[15] Twenty-five are in Africa, six in Latin America, eleven in Asia (including populous China, India, Pakistan and Indonesia) and one in Oceania. No doubt a very large percentage of the over 70 less developed countries omitted because of data deficiencies would also fall within type 1. In addition there are included 3 of the poorer countries of southern and southeastern Europe (Fig. 5.2).

Type 4 (high urbanization; 40 percent or more) includes 23 countries, all but three (Venezuela, Chile, and Cuba) of which belong in the more

[15] Data for this urban typology are from U.N., *World Survey,* 1965, supplemented by U.N., *Urban and Rural Population Growth,* 1967.

developed realm. Ten are in Europe, two in Anglo-America, five in Latin America, four in Asia and two in Oceania.

Based on large cities of 100,000+ population, Australia and Argentina are the world's two most highly urbanized countries. On first thought it may seem odd that in these Southern Hemisphere regions, where agricultural land is so outstandingly the basic resource and agricultural products represent such a large share of the exports, urbanization should be at such a high level. It reflects several features, including (1) the

TABLE 5.11 Estimates of Total and Urban Population for the Regions of the World, Around 1960

	Total Population (thousands)	Population in Places of 20,000 or more Inhabitants (thousands)	Percent of Total Population in Places of 20,000 or More Inhabitants
World total	2,990,000	712,000–745,000	24–25
Less developed regions	2,137,000	362,000–395,000	17–18
Africa	273,000	36,600	13
North Africa	66,000	17,400	26
Sub-Sahara Africa	207,000	19,200	9
Asia	1,651,000	257,000–290,000	16–18
Excluding China (Mainland)	1,001,000	192,000	19
China (Mainland)	650,000	65,000–97,500	10–15
Latin America	212,000	68,700	32
Argentina, Chile, Uruguay	31,000	17,400	56
Remainder of Latin America	181,000	51,300	28
More developed regions	853,000	350,000	41
North America	199,000	92,000	46
Europe (excluding U.S.S.R.)	425,000	171,000	40
Northwestern	142,000	77,000	54
Central	139,000	55,000	40
Southern	144,000	39,000	27
U.S.S.R.	214,000	78,000	36
Oceania	15,700	8,400	53
Australia and New Zealand	12,700	8,300	65
Remainder of Oceania	3,000	100	3

SOURCE: U.N., *World Survey*, 1965.

TABLE 5.12   Availability of Data on Population in Places of 20,000 or More Inhabitants, for Regions of the World Around 1960

	Number of Countries with Population of 250,000 or More		Population in Countries for which Data are Available [a]	
	Total Countries	Countries for which Data on Population in Places of 20,000 or More are Available [a]	Number (thousands)	Percentage of Population of Region
World total	152	90	1,867,255	62
Less developed regions	116	56	1,016,990	48
Africa	48	30	167,872	62
North Africa	6	6 [b]	65,955	100
Sub-Sahara Africa	42	24	101,917	49
Asia	41	11	678,209	41
Excluding China (Mainland)	40	11	678,209	68
China (Mainland)	1	—	—	—
Latin America	27	15	170,909	80
Argentina, Chile, Uruguay	3	2 [c]	28,583	92
Remainder of Latin America	24	13	142,326	78
More developed regions	36	34	850,265	100
North America	2	2	198,585	100
Europe (excluding U.S.S.R.)	28	28	424,199	100
Northwestern Europe	12	12	142,045	100
Central Europe	7	7	138,448	100
Southern Europe	9	9	143,706	100
U.S.S.R.	1	1	214,400	100
Oceania	5	3	13,081	83
Australia and New Zealand	2	2	12,687	100
Remainder of Oceania	3	1	394	13 [d]

SOURCE: U.N., *World Survey*, 1965.

[a] Excluding a few countries for which examination of available data had not been completed at the time of preparation of the present document.

extensive nature of much of the agriculture which requires a minimum of manpower, (2) a manufacturing structure based mainly upon the processing of agricultural products, and (3) a service structure which emphasizes financing, banking, and shipping of raw or processed products from the land (see Table 5.14).

Of the two intermediate urbanization types, type 2 (medium-low urbanization; 20–30 percent) includes 21 countries, 17 of which qualify as less developed. In type 3 (medium-high urbanization; 30–40 percent), of the 20 countries included, 11 are European, including the U.S.S.R., while 9 are usually classed as less developed. It is these intermediate types which are least homogeneous.

ECONOMIC WELL-BEING

Perhaps the best measure of a population's economic development and well-being is its average per capita national income. The range in per capita incomes among the world's countries is indeed large—from lows of $30 to $40 in some African countries to a high of nearly $2900 in the United States, and even over $3000 in oil-rich Kuwait, in eastern Arabia. Within this wide range there is a strong concentration of the less developed countries at the low end of the income scale. The spread of incomes is much wider among the more developed countries, but the average per capita national income is much higher (see Fig. 5.4). By this index the earth's traditional societies are usually those that fail to provide acceptable standards of living for a large proportion of their populations, with resulting widespread poverty and material deprivation.

Regrettably, however, average per capita national income fails to indicate the degree to which a nation's wealth is diffused throughout the whole population. In reality, the crucial test of economic well-being is the extent to which mass poverty is eliminated. But in some nations of considerable affluence, large proportions of their populations are still destitute and in want.

The salient feature of the map showing world distribution of average per capita national incomes is the contrast between the economically

---

b Data for the United Arab Republic partly estimated.

c Data for Argentina partly estimated.

d Islands having less than 250,000 population account for nearly one-fourth of the total population of this subregion. Recent census data are available for most of these islands, and, if included, the regional coverage would be about 35 percent.

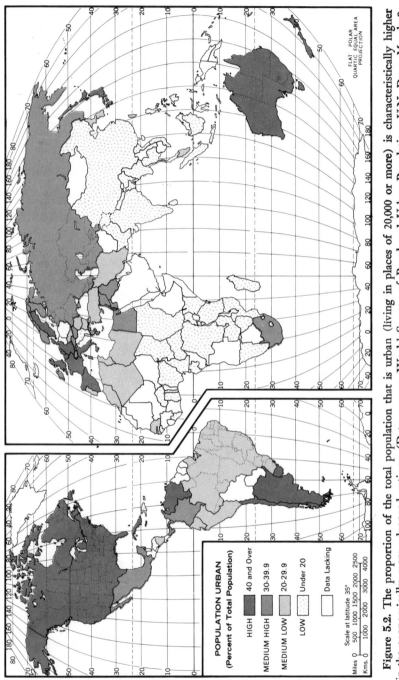

Figure 5.2. The proportion of the total population that is urban (living in places of 20,000 or more) is characteristically higher in the economically more advanced nations. (Data sources, World Survey of Rural and Urban Population, U.N. Doc., March 8, 1965; Urban and Rural Population Growth, 1920–1960 with Projections, U.N. Working Paper No. 15, Sept., 1967.)

TABLE 5.13 Percentages of Population in Places of 20,000 or More Inhabitants for the Regions of the World, 1950–1960

	Estimated Averages for All Countries			Averages for Countries Having 1950 and 1960 Data		
	1950	1960	Percent Increase in Proportion Urban[a]	1950	1960	Percent Increase in Proportion Urban[a]
World total	21	24–25[b]	12–17[b]	27	30	12
Less developed regions	14	17–18[b]	17–28[b]	18	22	19
Africa	10	13	37	14	18	27
North Africa	21	26	23	25	31	23
Sub-Sahara Africa	6	9	50	8	11	35
Asia	14	16–18[b]	11–26[b]	19	21	14
Excluding China (Mainland)	17	19	15	19	21	14
China (Mainland)	10	10–15[b]	0–50[b]	—	—	—
Latin America	25	32	28	28	36	29
Argentina, Chile, Uruguay	47	56	19	48	57	20
Remainder of Latin America	21	28	33	21	29	40
More developed regions	37	41	10	38	41	10
North America	43	46	6	43	46	6
Europe (excluding U.S.S.R.)	37	40	8	37	40	8
Northwestern	52	54	3	52	54	3
Central	37	40	9	37	40	9
Southern	23	27	16	23	27	16
U.S.S.R.	31	36	17	31	36	17
Remainder of Oceania	—	3	—	—	15	—
Oceania	46	53	15	56	64	13
Australia and New Zealand	58	65	12	58	65	12

SOURCE: U.N., *World Survey*, 1965.

[a] Computed from unrounded data.

[b] Range of estimated values corresponding to alternative estimates for China (Mainland).

TABLE 5.14   Percentage of Total Population Living in Cities of 100,000 or more (early 1960s)

United States	51
England and Wales	50
Canada	45
Japan	44
Argentina	56
Uruguay	43
Australia	60
New Zealand	44
Iraq	51

SOURCE: *U.N. Demographic Yearbook, 1965.*

less developed and more developed realms (Fig. 5.3). The dichotomy is not complete, however, for some half dozen countries in southern and southeastern Europe have incomes as low as or even lower than some others that are classed as traditional societies (Fig. 5.4).

In the more developed realm the range of incomes is large. Highest is that of Anglo-America, followed in order by Oceania, Europe, and U.S.S.R. The latter's per capita productivity is less than one-third that of the United States. Europe shows a particularly large spread of per capita national incomes, for whereas western and northern Europe's are high (usually between $1000 and $1500), eastern and southern Europe's are only one-half to one-third as great (Table 5.15 and Fig. 5.3).

TABLE 5.15   Average Per Capita National Incomes, about 1965, in U.S. Dollars

World	493
Anglo-America	2,793
Europe	1,069
U.S.S.R.	928
Oceania	1,636
Africa	123
Asia	128
Latin America	344

SOURCE: *World Population Data Sheet—1968.*

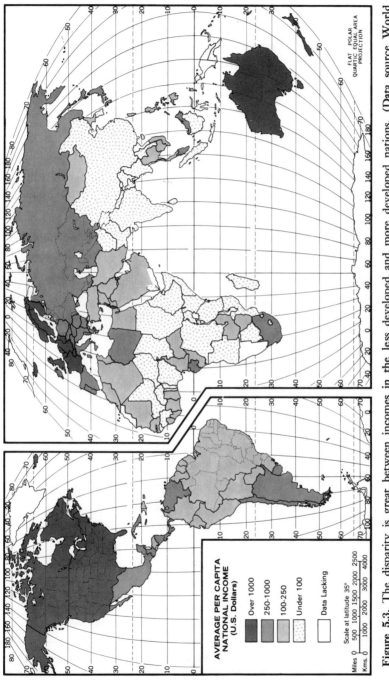

Figure 5.3. The disparity is great between incomes in the less developed and more developed nations. (Data source World Population Data Sheet—1968.)

165

The three less developed continents have incomes that are well below the world average and of course far less than that of any one of the more developed continents (Fig. 5.4). Africa and Asia are not only lowest on the scale, but they are also remarkably similar in their low per capita productivity. Latin America is two to three times as high. In large part this reflects the overall greater economic advancement of Latin America

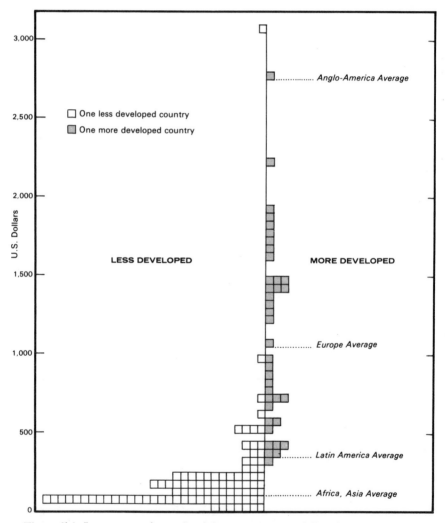

Figure 5.4. Low per capita national incomes are especially characteristic of the economically less developed countries. There is a wide range of incomes among the more developed countries. (Data source World Population Sheet—1968.)

within the triumvirate of less developed continents; in lesser degree it is caused by the inclusion of Argentina and Uruguay, which are patently not less developed countries. As a general rule, the Latin American countries fronting on the Caribbean have higher incomes than those in tropical South America south of the equator. In Africa it is mainly the countries at the northern and southern extremities, and a few in equatorial West Africa, that show the highest incomes. In Asia it is Southwest Asia, and Malaysia and the Philippines in the southeast, that rise somewhat above the general continental low level of production.

ECONOMIC COMPOSITION

Like the feature of rural or urban residence described earlier, economic composition is not in itself a characteristic of population. It is recognized, nevertheless, that an individual's occupational status does influence his personality, social outlook, political allegiance, and ways of thinking, and when employment affects large groups of people certain population characteristics may be the result. Yet economic character is an elusive population feature, for there is bound to be a wide range of social and economic levels represented within the broad categories that must be used in any worldwide comparisons.

The total population of a country may be subdivided into that part which is economically active and that which is inactive. The economically active group is sometimes spoken of as the *labor force*, or the working population. It is defined as not only those men and women who are actually engaged in productive employment, but also those who may be only temporarily unemployed. Included are employers, employees, the self-employed, unpaid family workers, domestic servants, and members of the armed forces. The inactive group is composed of children, retired persons, students, housewives, inmates of institutions, and those living from royalties, rents, pensions, dividends, etc.

In economically advanced nations like the United States and many of those in Europe, much time and money are expended in collecting and publishing detailed data on the working population, including employment status, occupation, and economic composition. But comparably abundant and detailed data have not been collected for much of the earth's poorer populations, so that worldwide societal comparisons of economic characteristics are limited. Data on such items as size and efficiency of a labor force, the fractional part unemployed, and the proportions employed in different economic sectors are of unusual importance to a wide variety of business and government agencies.

TABLE 5.16   Male Activity Rates by Age Groups (per 100 Males)
Observed in or About 1950 in Three Groups of Countries
Classified by Level of Economic Development

		Age Groups							
Countries	All Ages	10–14	15–19	20–24	25–34	35–44	45–54	55–64	65 and Over
Underdeveloped	58.5	30.8	81.8	93.1	96.2	97.2	96.2	90.7	78.5
Semideveloped	57.3	8.6	70.9	91.8	96.1	97.1	96.0	90.0	62.5
Developed	61.5	4.9	68.9	90.7	96.2	97.2	94.9	83.5	40.6

SOURCE: U.N., *Population Studies* No. 26, p. 52.

NOTE: The criterion for the above classification of countries is here taken
as the percentage of males employed in agriculture: underdeveloped
60 percent or over, semideveloped 35–59 percent, and developed less
than 35 percent.

The Labor Force. The proportion of a population that is economically active is an important variable for international comparison. But
diverse national definitions and age limits make such comparisons difficult. Age structure is one important determinant of the proportion of
a population which is economically active. As pointed out in an earlier
section, most less developed countries are economically burdened by an
abnormally large proportion of children, and some advanced countries
by a large proportion of aged, both of these groups composed largely of
economically inactive individuals. But the effects of these features are
complicated by the fact that in the less developed countries, where agriculture is the dominant economy, a larger fraction of both the young
and the aged are economically active (see Table 5.16).

Various other factors influence the proportions who are economically
active; among them are age of marriage, levels of income, average size
of family, and state of health.

Industrial Composition. Based upon type of establishment, product
made, or service rendered, thousands of different industries are recognized. For the sake of convenience in international comparisons the
United Nations Statistical Commission has reduced this long list to nine
main groups:

1. Agriculture, forestry, hunting, and fishing.
2. Mining and quarrying.

3. Manufacturing.
4. Construction.
5. Production of gas and electricity.
6. Commerce.
7. Transport, storage, and communication.
8. Services.
9. All others.

For many comparisons among countries these nine are combined into three general groups of economic activity:

1. *Primary activities*—agriculture, forestry, hunting and fishing, mining and quarrying.
2. *Secondary activities*—manufacturing, construction and electricity, gas and water workers.
3. *Tertiary activities*—commerce, transportation, storage, and communication; and service workers of all kinds.

Although the threefold division is crude, resulting in overlappings of activities into more than one group, it does serve usefully to differentiate the earth's societies.

Figure 5.5 showing the percent of the economically active population engaged in *primary* activities (mainly agricultural) reveals some very basic patterns of large-scale dimensions. Normally the population group engaged in primary activities declines in relative importance as a country advances economically, for the other expanding economic sectors must recruit their labor from the farms. In most of the advanced countries the agricultural population has declined relatively since the late 1800s or early 1900s; absolute decline was postponed until recent decades. The main polarization is between the less developed nations with their high proportions of the labor force engaged in the primary economic sector, preponderantly agriculture, and the more developed countries in which the proportions are low. In most of the less developed realm the proportion in primary industries is over 50 percent. Balkan Europe also looms high in the proportion of its labor force employed in the primary sector. In numerous countries in Africa and Asia the proportion exceeds 70 percent. Of the three less developed continents, the proportion is lowest in tropical Latin America.

At the opposite extreme are United States and the United Kingdom with only 8 and 9 percent of their labor forces engaged in primary activities. To be sure, in most of the economically advanced countries these figures are exceeded, but in a large number they are under 25 percent. Anglo-America, western Europe, Australia, New Zealand, Argentina, and Uruguay belong in this class.

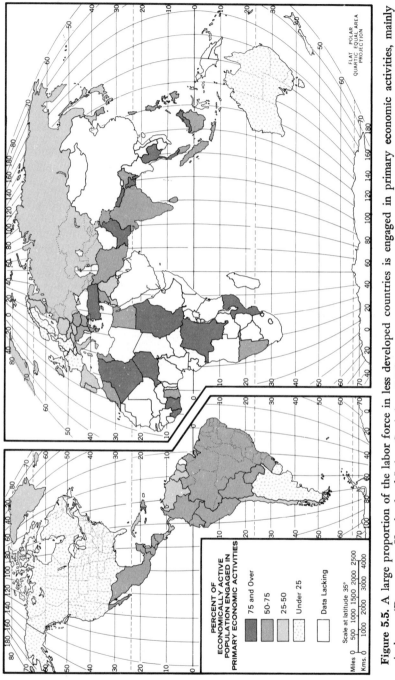

Figure 5.5. A large proportion of the labor force in less developed countries is engaged in primary economic activities, mainly agriculture. (Data source Yearbook of Labor Statistics, 1965.)

PERCENT OF
ECONOMICALLY ACTIVE
POPULATION ENGAGED IN
PRIMARY ECONOMIC ACTIVITIES

75 and Over
50-75
25-50
Under 25
Data Lacking

Scale at latitude 35°

Miles 0 500 1000 1500 2000 2500
Kms. 0 1000 2000 3000 4000

FLAT POLAR
QUARTIC EQUAL AREA
PROJECTION

Between the two extremes is a varied assortment of countries with mixed economies and intermediate proportions of their labor forces in the primary sector. It includes the U.S.S.R., Japan, Austria, Poland, Czechoslovakia, Finland, Ireland, and Chile.

The secondary economic sector produces material goods. An increasing relative proportion of the total population engaged in manufacturing and construction is characteristic of the modern world. Such a situation is a symbol of economic metamorphosis in which there is an increasing use of machines and mechanical power. The trend in the proportion of world population engaged in secondary industry is definitely upward. This increase appears to be finite, however, for saturation has apparently been reached in some countries. In the United Kingdom, for example, the proportion has been nearly static since about 1911.

Distributional aspects of the proportion of the labor force engaged in secondary industries is rather the reverse of that for the primary sector—high proportions are identified with the advanced countries, and low proportions with the less developed (Fig. 5.6). Proportions of 35 percent and over are achieved in some 10 countries in western, central, and Mediterranean Europe. The two Southern Hemisphere countries of Australia and New Zealand are also included in this high-percentage group. But relatively high ratios of 25 to 35 percent are typical of more extensive areas—Anglo-America, most of the rest of Europe except the Balkans, Soviet Russia, Japan, Argentina and Uruguay.

Although the average proportion of the labor force engaged in the secondary industries in the less developed realm is low, the spread between the individual countries is large. They vary from as low as 1 percent and under in a few states of sub-Sahara Africa to over 20 percent in half a dozen countries in Latin America. Ten percent or less is probably characteristic of most of black Africa and parts of Southeast, South and Southwest Asia, including populous Pakistan and Indonesia. Under 15 percent also includes populous India. Fifteen to 25 percent is typical of Latin America, much of Southwest Asia, and the Balkan Peninsula in Europe.

Tertiary industry represents a highly composite group of activities; as a class it is not responsible for the production of material goods but for a great variety of services. Tertiary industry includes activities which are poles apart insofar as they represent social-economic status and wealth. At one extreme is domestic service and petty shopkeeping; at the other is the huge insurance company, mercantile establishment, and bank. The more primitive forms of tertiary occupation characterize less developed countries. Its complex and sophisticated forms are a part of the civilization of the most advanced societies.

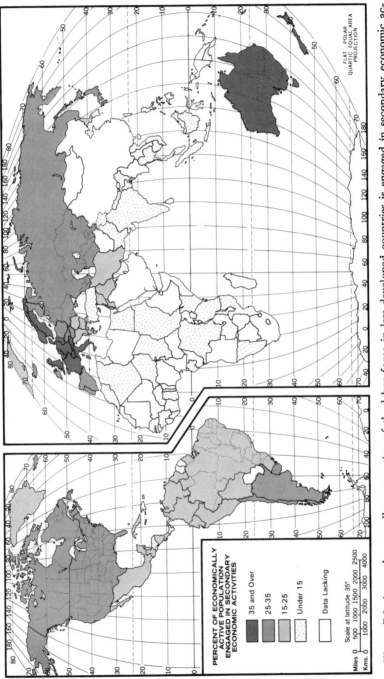

Figure 5.6. As a rule, a smaller proportion of the labor force in less developed countries is engaged in secondary economic activities (manufacturing, construction, etc.) than is the case in the more affluent ones. (Data source same as for Fig. 5.5.)

PERCENT OF ECONOMICALLY ACTIVE POPULATION ENGAGED IN SECONDARY ECONOMIC ACTIVITIES

35 and Over

25-35

15-25

Under 15

Data Lacking

Scale at latitude 35°

Miles 0   500 1000 1500 2000 2500

Kms. 0   1000 2000 3000 4000

FLAT POLAR QUARTIC EQUAL AREA PROJECTION

Workers engaged in tertiary activity represent an expanding sector in the world's population, for their services tend to grow along with industrialization and urbanization. The nature of the tertiary activity evolves and is transformed as it expands. For while growth of the secondary sector represents mainly a strengthening of the economic potential of a country, a large increment in tertiary activities, leading to a well-balanced tertiary group, points to a high degree of national sophistication and a flowering of national personality. In the evolution of tertiary activities three lines of progress are evident:

1. Extension of public services as the state increasingly looks after the welfare of its citizens.
2. Improvement of the communication-transport services which makes regional specialization and large-scale industry possible.
3. Progress in trade and finance to serve the increasingly complex needs of an affluent society.

The United States and Canada lead the world in emphasis on the tertiary sector, 55 and 53 percent of their working populations being so engaged (Fig. 5.7). This is probably the first time in history that a country's workers rendering services exceed in numbers those producing material goods. In these two countries, the labor requirements of administration, supervision, and control exceed those of material production—strong evidence of the unusual economic complexity and sophistication prevailing in Anglo-America. Also high in the proportion of the labor force engaged in tertiary occupations is a group of some dozen countries in western Europe, as well as Israel, Australia and New Zealand, and Uruguay, Venezuela, Puerto Rico, and Surinam in Latin America. At the opposite extreme with low proportions in tertiary activities, are most of the less developed countries, although, to be sure, data are lacking for a goodly number in Africa and Asia. Expectedly, the proportions are especially low in Africa, where some countries fall below 10 percent. Ten to 30 percent is more characteristic of the less developed regions as a whole, with Latin America higher on the average than Asia and Africa. Balkan Europe is as low as many less developed countries. Perhaps the chief surprise is U.S.S.R. with only about 20 percent engaged in the tertiary occupations. In part this reflects the purposeful emphasis placed upon the production of material goods in order to make the country economically and militarily strong. Somewhat intermediate (30–40 percent) in emphasis on the tertiary sector are a few widely scattered countries—some half a dozen in Europe, and also Japan, Argentina, Chile and Brazil.

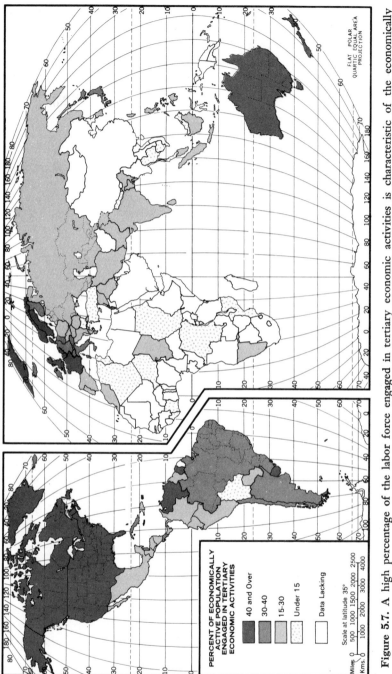

Figure 5.7. A high percentage of the labor force engaged in tertiary economic activities is characteristic of the economically more affluent nations. Tertiary activities are poorly represented in Africa, large parts of Asia, and tropical Latin America. (Data sources same as for Fig. 5.5.)

PERCENT OF ECONOMICALLY ACTIVE POPULATION ENGAGED IN TERTIARY ECONOMIC ACTIVITIES

40 and Over
30-40
15-30
Under 15
Data Lacking

Scale at latitude 35°

Miles 0 500 1000 1500 2000 2500
Kms. 0 1000 2000 3000 4000

FLAT POLAR QUARTIC EQUAL AREA PROJECTION

174

REFERENCES

Marital Status

Clarke, John I. *Population Geography*. Pergamon Press, Oxford, 1965. Pp. 76–79.

Smith, T. Lynn. *Fundamentals of Population Study*. Lippincott, Philadelphia, Pa., 1960. Pp. 212–228.

Thomlinson, Ralph. *Population Dynamics*. Random House, New York, 1965. Pp. 457–464.

Education and Literacy; Language and Religion

Bottiglioni, G. "Linguistic Geography: Its Achievements, Methods and Orientations," *Word*, 1954, pp. 375–387.

Broek, Jan O. M., and John W. Webb. *A Geography of Mankind*. McGraw-Hill, New York, 1968. Pp. 97–122; 124–151.

Bruk, S. I. and V. S. Aperchenko (eds.). *Atlas Narodov Mira* (*Atlas of the People of the World*). Moscow, 1964.

Fleure, H. J. "The Geographical Distribution of the Major Religions," *Bulletin de la Société Royale de Géographie d'Egypte*, Vol. 24, 1951, pp. 1–18.

Sopher, D. E. *The Geography of Religions*. Prentice-Hall, Englewood Cliffs, N. J., 1967.

Smith, T. Lynn. *Fundamentals of Population Study*. Lippincott, Philadelphia, Pa., 1960. Pp. 251–268.

Thomlinson, Ralph. *Population Dynamics*. Random House, New York, 1965. Pp. 464–472.

UNESCO Statistical Division. *World Illiteracy at Mid-Century*. Monographs on Fundamental Education, Paris, 1957.

United Nations. *Report on the World Social Situation*. New York, 1957. Pp. 64–90.

Mobility and Migration

Beaujeu-Garnier, J. *Geography of Population*. St. Martin's Press, New York, 1966. Pp. 167–281.

Clarke, John I. *Population Geography*. Pergamon, Oxford, 1965. Pp. 123–137.

Heberle, Rudolf. "Types of Migration," *Research Group for European Migration Problems. Bulletin*, Vol. 4, No. 1, January–March 1956, pp. 1–5.

Petersen, William. "A General Typology of Migration," *Am. Sociol. Rev.*, Vol. 23, No. 3, June 1958. Pp. 256–266.

Petersen, William. *Population*. Macmillan, New York, 1961. Pp. 529–621 (2nd ed. 1969).

Sorre, M. *Les Migrations des Peuples*. Flammarion, Paris, 1955.

Smith, T. Lynn. *Fundamentals of Population Study*. Lippincott, Philadelphia, Pa., 1960. Pp. 417–488.

Taft, D. R., and R. Robbins. *Internation Migrations: The Immigrant in the Modern World*. Ronald Press, New York, 1955.

Residence: Rural-Urban

Clarke, John I. *Population Geography*. Pergamon, Oxford, 1965. Pp. 45–61.

Davis, Kingsley. "The Urbanization of the Human Population," *Scientific American*, Vol. 213, September 1965. Pp. 41–53.

Davis, Kingsley, and Hilda Hertz. "The World Distribution of Urbanization," *Bulletin of the International Statistical Institute*, Vol. 33, No. 4, 1954, pp. 227–243.

Duncan, Otis Dudley, and A. J. Reiss. *Social Characteristics of Urban and Rural Communities, 1950*. Wiley, New York, 1956.

Ginsberg, Norton. Urban Population. In *Atlas of Economic Development*. University of Chicago Press, Chicago, 1961. Pp. 34–37.

Hawley, Amos H. World Urbanization: Trends and Prospects. In Ronald Freedman (ed.), *Population: The Vital Revolution*, Aldine, Chicago, 1965. Pp. 70–83.

Hoyt, Homer. *World Urbanization: Expanding Population in a Shrinking World*. Urban Land Institute, Technical Bulletin No. 43, Washington, D.C., 1962.

Mumford, Lewis. *The City in History*. Harcourt, Brace and World, New York, 1961.

Petersen, William. *Population*. Macmillan, New York, 1961. Pp. 179–208.

Smith, T. Lynn. *Fundamentals of Population Study*. Lippincott, Philadelphia, Pa., 1960. Pp. 75–108.

Thomlinson, Ralph. *Population Dynamics*. Random House, New York, 1965. Pp. 271–299.

United Nations. *Report on the World Social Situation*. New York, 1957. Pp. 111–192.

United Nations, Economic and Social Council. *World Survey of Rural and Urban Population Growth*. Doc. E/CN.9/187, March 8, 1965.

United Nations, Population Division. *Urban and Rural Population Growth, 1920–1960 with Projections*. Working Paper No. 15, September, 1967. 144 pp.

Weber, Adna Ferrin. *The Growth of Cities in the Nineteenth Century*. Cornell University Press, Ithaca, N.Y., 1963.

The World's Metropolitan Areas. University of California Press, 1959.

Economic Composition

Beaujeu-Garnier, J. *Geography of Population*. St. Martins Press, New York, 1966. Pp. 285–332.

Clarke, John I. *Population Geography*. Pergamon, Oxford, 1965. Pp. 84–93.

Smith, T. Lynn. *Fundamentals of Population Study*. Lippincott, Philadelphia, Pa., 1960. Pp. 229–250.

Thomlinson, Ralph. *Population Dynamics*. Random House, New York, 1965. Pp. 472–484.

United Nations. *Report on the World Social Situation, 1957*. See Chap. VI, Conditions of Work and Employment, pp. 91–110.

Woytinsky, W. S., and E. S. Woytinsky. *World Population and Production: Trends and Outlook*. Twentieth Century Fund, New York, 1953.

Index

Accelerated population growth, by continents, 29
  in less developed regions, 31
  in modern period, 28–39
  in more developed regions, 31
Africa, linguistic diversity in, 134
  mortality rates in, 108–110
  population in, c. 1650, 22
    c. 1850, 61–62
    in early Christian Era, 18–19
  population change in, after c. 1850, 69
  population growth, 1750–1950, 32
  population growth rates in, 53
  stage in demographic transition, 47
  urbanization in, 151
Age groups, 119–122
  adult, 122–123
  aged, 122, 126
  youthful, 122, 125
Age indexes, 123–124
Age pyramid(s), 99, 119–121
  asymmetries in, 119
  irregularities in, 119
  of less developed countries, 119
  of more developed countries, 119
  shapes of, 119
  two general types of, 119–121
Age-specific death rate, 108
Age structure, 117–127
  determinants of, 118–119
  effects on, of birth rate, 118
    of death rate, 118
    of migration, 118–119, 137
  factors influencing, 117–118
  implications of, 118
  significance of, 117
  typology of, 124–125
  world patterns of, 124–127
    of aged, 126
    of youth, 125
Age structure data, uses of, 117
Agricultural Revolution, 6–9
  effects of, on population density, 8
    on population growth, 6–9
    on population redistribution, 8–9
Agriculture, beginnings of, 6–9

Americas, population of, in preurban period, 9–11
  pre-Columbian population of, 24–26
Ancient man, origins of, 5
Ancient world, China's population in, 15
  India's population in, 15
  population in, 12–19
  population in three great empires, 12–18
Ancient world's population, 12–19
  Africa, 18–19
  Americas, 18–19
  China, 15
  Europe, 17–19
  India, 15
  Middle East, 17
  Roman Empire, 15–17
Anglo-America, growth rates in, 53
  modern population distribution in, 67–68
Asia, mortality rates in, 108–110
  population change in, after c. 1850, 69
  population growth, 1750–1950, 32
  population growth rates in, 53
  population in, c. 1650, 21–22
    c. 1850, 59–60
Asia's population, vegetarian diet of, 89–90
Asia's population clusters, unusual features of, 89–90
Australia, population of, c. 1850, 63
Australoids, 94–95

Beloch's population figures, 18
Biological population characteristics, 93–127
Birth control, 97
  in less developed countries, 102
  necessity for, 34–35
Birth rate(s), crude, 97
  effects on age structure, 118
  world range of, 98–99

Caucasoid race, 94–95
Caucasoids, Europeans, 94–95
  Indo-Iranians, 94–95

179